A volume of a series in religion, edited by
LUTHER A. WEIGLE, STERLING PROFESSOR OF
RELIGIOUS EDUCATION AND DEAN, YALE UNIVERSITY
DIVINITY SCHOOL; *and* CLARENCE P. SHEDD,
STEPHEN MERRELL CLEMENT PROFESSOR OF CHRISTIAN METHODS, YALE UNIVERSITY DIVINITY SCHOOL

UNDERSTANDING CHRISTIANITY

A STUDY OF OUR CHRISTIAN HERITAGE

By

EDGAR M. McKOWN, Ph.D.

DEAN, EVANSVILLE COLLEGE
EVANSVILLE, INDIANA

and

CARL J. SCHERZER, B.D.

CHAPLAIN, PROTESTANT DEACONESS HOSPITAL
EVANSVILLE, INDIANA

THE RONALD PRESS COMPANY · NEW YORK

PREFACE

Understanding Christianity deals with basic questions now in the minds of students concerning the nature of the Christian faith and the implications of that faith for the issues of today. It has been written to supply a need we have felt increasingly in our teaching of courses in the Christian religion: the need for a book presenting basic Christian beliefs in a manner understandable to young people, one that will stimulate them to further thought, reading, and discussion. A second conscious objective has been to present this material with a simplicity and a challenge that will bring actively into class discussions those students who have little actual religious education and background.

While *Understanding Christianity* is designed for use as a guide in college or nursing classes in religion, it can also be used by study groups in churches, YMCAs, or other similar organizations. We have found that such classes or groups are very much interested in those aspects of the Christian religion presented here. Because the material is presented simply and coherently, *Understanding Christianity* should prove of comparable value to the individual who seeks to become better acquainted with Christian thought and beliefs.

Two things we feel to be of particular importance:

First, in seeking the meaning of Christianity we should not only talk about the Bible, we should *use* it as well. Because many nurtured in the churches today are unfamiliar with the Bible (in too many cases, lesson materials have become a substitute), *Understanding Christianity* sends the reader directly to the Bible. To achieve this, relevant scriptural material is not quoted in the text; instead, specific references are given in footnotes. Searching out these citations will not only supplement the text, it will familiarize the reader with the contents of the various books of the Bible.

Second, this book is intended to serve as a starting point that will provoke thought and stimulate further independent reading. A sufficiently interested student can expand his knowledge and understanding of these religious foundations by reading a history of the Church, or he can devote himself to some of the many stimulating books that probe deeply into the problems of the Church today. Several of each are suggested in the Bibliography.

As to the content itself, we have sought to discuss those subjects that most Christians, regardless of denomination, think about seriously. It is natural that, in such an approach, some issues must be presented about which there is a difference of opinion. We have attempted to present such material in a manner as unbiased as possible. Finally, appreciating the vital character of their contributions, we have incorporated the ideas of a number of outstanding Christian thinkers as they relate to the subject discussed. The Bibliography is a recognition of this obligation.

It is our hope that this book will inspire the reader to continue his study of our rich religious heritage and will encourage him to personal religious living.

EDGAR M. McKOWN
CARL J. SCHERZER

Evansville, Indiana
    December, 1948

CONTENTS

v

CONTENTS

UNDERSTANDING CHRISTIANITY

CHAPTER 1

How May We Use the Bible?

Millions of copies of the Bible are printed and sold each year. It is the best seller. "Year by year in the centers of culture it sells more copies than any best seller in its brief day." [1] People read it in many languages. However, many are baffled by what use to make of the Bible. It raises unanswered questions in the minds of many persons. The purpose of this chapter is to give a background which may aid in a modern interpretation of the Bible.

A. How the Bible Came to Be

The Bible has been called the Book of Life. It is about living people, and it is therefore helpful to us in living. We can be helped to realize this by noting some of the life situations in which the books of the Bible originated.

THE WRITTEN WORD OF GOD.—About the middle of the eighth century before Christ, a person named Amos who lived south of Bethlehem in Tekoa went to the wealthy cities of the North to sell his produce. There he was astonished by the business practices. Money was loaned at high rates of interest. Merchants bought crops and produce, using measures and weights which did not honestly indicate the value of the goods they were buying. The peasants borrowed at high rates of interest money which they could not repay. Having thus gotten into debt, they were compelled to give up ownership of their farms and to continue to work on them as slaves.

[1] H. F. Rall, *A Faith for Today*, Abingdon-Cokesbury Press, 1936, p. 224.

Amos condemned this greed and injustice. He was accused of plotting against the king. Having been denied the ears of the people, he returned home and wrote a book. He hoped that his teachings might thus be preserved for a time when their consideration would be more favorable. The book of Amos is the first book of the Bible completed in its present form.

Over a century later, in the year 622 B.C., workmen were renovating the temple at Jerusalem in a reform instituted by King Josiah. Under King Manasseh the nation had just passed through a period of distress for the worshipers of Jehovah in which prophets had been martyred. Josiah, however, sought to restore the worship of the God of Israel. The workmen found a book hidden in the temple [2] which evidently had been written during the dark days of the reign of Manasseh. It was taken to the prophetess Huldah, who declared it to be the Word of God. This is the first time in Hebrew history that the Word of God came to them first in written form. It was used by Josiah as the basis for further reform. The beginning of the Jewish Scriptures, it is found in our Bible in Deuteronomy, chapters 12–24, and chapter 26.

HISTORY.—A quarter of a century after the appearance of the book of Deuteronomy, the people of Judah were carried away as exiles to Babylon. Just as scholars always are careful to preserve records and literary treasures, so it was in this case. Books of history, along with the records of the royal court, were taken to Babylon. It is also true that, when a crisis comes in the national life, history is rewritten. This was true in the case of the Hebrews. The history of the Israelite nation was rewritten in Babylon to show their children that when the Israelites obeyed God they were prosperous and that when they disobeyed Him they were punished. These books are our present books of Samuel and Kings

[2] II Kings 22:8–20.

There were hero stories also, stories of Samson, stories of Deborah, of Jephthah, and others. Introductions were written for these stories, and sometimes postscripts, to point out to the reader that when the Israelites obeyed God they were prosperous and when they turned away from Him they were punished. Among the books of history taken to Babylon was a history of Judah written about 650 B.C. and known to modern scholars as J. A history of Israel had been written about 750 B.C. which is known to scholars as E. A compilation was made that included these two histories, the book of Deuteronomy, some poems, and court records. During the Bablyonian Captivity the scholars were busy.

THE LAW.—During this period the priests came more and more into power. They wrote certain regulations for worship and practices of religion; the last chapters of the book of Ezekiel and most of the book of Leviticus were written to provide regulations which would prevent the Israelites from violating the will of God. After they returned once more to their own land and the temple was built and the national life restored, the priestly writings were combined with the compilation of J and E and Deuteronomy. We know these writings now as Genesis, Exodus, Leviticus, Numbers, and Deuteronomy. It is believed that this is what Ezra read [3] to the Israelites and established as the Law of the Jewish nation at the beginning of the fourth century before Christ. Thus we have the story of the formation of the first Jewish Scriptures—the Law.

THE PROPHETS.—A century or two later the Jewish people realized that there were no more prophets among them, and the addition of the writings of the prophets to their Scriptures gained in favor. These included the writings of Isaiah, a prince who lived in Jerusalem in the latter half of the eighth

[3] Nehemiah 8:1-8.

century before Christ. He was very close to the kings of his day and had a great deal of influence on the decisions of the rulers, and therefore upon the history of the nation. To his writings have been added those of others.

The prophets also included Jeremiah who vainly pleaded with the rulers not to make an alliance with Babylon. When they nevertheless made the alliance, he again pleaded with them not to break it. He had the misfortune of seeing his advice unheeded and disaster brought upon the nation. Tradition says that he died at the hands of his fellow countrymen in Egypt, where he had been taken against his will. His writings show a noble type of religious experience.

Among the prophetic writings is the book of Ezekiel. Ezekiel was a young priest of Jerusalem who was carried away into captivity in Babylon when the Jews were taken into exile. There he rapidly adjusted himself to the new conditions and helped his fellow exiles to keep their chins up during the early years of their captivity.

The prophets also included a number of prophetic books referred to as "The Twelve." The book of Amos, to which we have already referred, was one of these.

The books of Joshua, of Judges, of Samuel, and of Kings were added to the prophets. They were the histories written from the prophet's point of view, and were called "the Former Prophets." The books of Isaiah, Jeremiah, Ezekiel, and the Twelve were called "the Latter Prophets." The Law and the Prophets constituted the Bible of Jesus' day. Jesus quoted from other Hebrew literature which may also have been considered sacred.

THE WRITINGS.—The Jews had a hymnbook of the Temple. Psalms had been written for use in the sanctuaries from the very earliest time in their history. They were collected into several hymnals. The collection to which the

Psalms belonged is indicated often in the title. You will note a Song of Korah, or a Song of Asaph. Finally these earlier collections were brought together into the book of Psalms as we now have it. Included are one hundred fifty Psalms divided into five books, as the Law is divided into five books.

The book of Psalms became part of another section of the Hebrew Scriptures known as "The Writings." The Writings included the books of Job, Proverbs, Ruth, and the rest of the books found in the King James version or American Standard version of the Old Testament, excluding, of course, those included in the Law and the Prophets as given above. These writings finally became a part of the sacred Scriptures of the Jews. The question of the sacredness of the books was finally settled at a synod held about the year 90 A.D. at Jamnia.

THE APOSTLE.—In the meantime the Christians were writing. The apostle Paul had visited some cities in Europe, notably Philippi, Thessalonica, and Athens. At Thessalonica he had left a few converts, when he was compelled to flee because of the hostility of some of his fellow countrymen.[4] When he finally arrived at Corinth he showed considerable anxiety about the ability of his converts to continue in their newly found faith. For some reason he found it impossible to return to Thessalonica; it may have been because of an illness or it may have been because he feared that his return would stir up more persecution and unnecessarily endanger the new converts. Instead, he chose to write a letter in which he discussed some of the matters which were causing them difficulty. This letter was soon followed by another. Later, when he had left Corinth, he wrote several letters to the Corinthians. During the course of his ministry he wrote similar letters to some seven or eight of the churches which he had established, giving directions, reprimand, or encourage-

[4] Acts 17:5–10.

ment, as the occasion required. These letters, collected about the year 90 A.D., were read in the church services.

THE GOSPELS AND THE BOOK OF ACTS.—Even before Paul wrote his Letter to the Thessalonians other Christians had written some of the stories about Jesus and his sayings to be used in teaching those who were coming into the Christian fold. Those who had known Jesus in the flesh were passing from the scene of action. The Christian leaders saw the necessity of preserving in writing their memories of what Jesus had done and said. According to tradition, Peter's death in 64 A.D. shocked the Christians into concern for such preservation. A few years after that Mark completed the Gospel which bears his name. The Gospel according to Matthew and the Gospel according to Luke followed ten to fifteen years later. Luke, who was a traveling companion of Paul, also wrote at that time the book of the Acts of the Apostles. This book may have been the occasion of the collection of Paul's letters. The Gospel of John was written about the end of the first century of the Christian era. Each of the Gospels was a compilation of earlier and briefer reports.

OTHER WRITINGS.—A number of other documents, mostly letters, appeared in this period, both during the years in which the above books were written, and during those that followed; many of these are now included in the New Testament. One of the latest New Testament books was written about the year 150, for the purpose of reviving the hope of the second coming of Christ. It is known to us as the Second Epistle of Peter. A reading of it reveals that it was written long after the Apostles were dead.[5] By this time Paul's letters had become Scripture.[6]

[5] II Peter 3:2.
[6] II Peter 3:15–16.

CHRISTIAN SCRIPTURES.—These early Christian writings were read in the churches; in fact, Paul's letter included directions that they be read in other churches.[7] However, for a considerable time there was no agreement as to which of the writings should be included in the Scriptures and which should not. Finally Athanasius, Bishop of Alexandria, wrote a letter to his diocese, Easter 367, in which he named the twenty-seven books we now have. About 400 A.D. Jerome completed the translation of the twenty-seven books on Athanasius' list into Latin; this version has commonly been called the Vulgate. These books, together with the Old Testament, have been accepted as the Christian Scriptures down to the present time.

This is an altogether inadequate account of how the Bible came to be, but it serves to indicate to us that it grew out of life situations of people like us, and that it is a deposit of the great religious moments and experiences of the race. The story of the preparation and preservation of the Bible is a thrilling one. It should add to the appreciation, if not to the value, of the Bible for the modern reader.

B. How the Bible Has Been Used

We may get some help in the use of the Bible by discussing Jesus' use of the Bible, the use which has been made by Christians through the centuries, and especially the use by our grandparents, the last generation in which there was widespread use of the Bible.

JESUS' USE OF THE BIBLE.—When Jesus was a boy of five He, like other Jewish boys of His time, learned the Shema.[8] When He was a man He used the Shema to answer a questioner [9] and gave us the great Christian commandment.

---

[7] Colossians 4:16.
[8] Deuteronomy 6:4. This is so called after the first Hebrew word in the passage, which means listen.
[9] Mark 12:29–31.

Jesus' teachings show familiarity with the law and the prophets, the Scriptures of His people which have become a part of the Christian Old Testament. According to the Gospels, He quoted one hundred thirty-four passages from twenty-four of the Old Testament books. Many of His expressions, while they are not exactly quotations, unquestionably indicate His familiarity with His Bible.

Jesus' use of the Scriptures may be helpful in planning the way we shall use them. He used the Scriptures to express His teachings. He may have learned from the Psalms that the meek inherit the earth.[10] He also used the words of the Psalms to express His own feelings. The most outstanding instance is His quotation on the Cross of Psalm 22:1.[11] Jesus' use of the Scriptures was selective. He sometimes quoted only part of a verse, omitting words which do not harmonize with His teachings. In the synagogue at Nazareth He quoted from Isaiah 61:1, 2. He did not quote the part of verse 2 which reads "the day of vengeance of our God." Evidently He thought that the world had seen enough of vengeance.[12] In fact, Jesus' teaching often indicates that his own thought has progressed beyond His Scriptures.[13] For some of the most inspiring and helpful passages in Jesus' sayings, we are indebted to the Scriptures.

THE EARLY CHURCH'S USE OF THE BIBLE.—In the early centuries the church, which was making converts from pagan religions, did not allow church members to make their own interpretation of the Scriptures. This was probably a very good thing since the converted pagans had no background, such as had the Jews to whom the Christian message first came. The Bible, therefore, had to be interpreted by those competent to interpret it. Thus interpreted, the Bible became one of the authorities of the Church.

[10] Matthew 5:5; Psalm 37:11.
[11] Matthew 27:46.
[12] Luke 4:18, 19.
[13] Matthew 5:21, 22.

THE PROTESTANT VIEW OF THE BIBLE.—After Europe
had been Christian for several centuries, such authority of
interpretation became unnecessary and translations of the
Scripture began to be made into the languages spoken by the
people. For the Protestant portion of Christianity the Bible
then became the supreme authority. It was considered an
infallible book. The exact words of the Bible were believed
to have been dictated by God. This is known as the doctrine
of verbal inspiration. It was felt necessary to study the Bible
in the languages which God had used, and so ministers
studied Hebrew and Greek. In more recent times, many laymen have mistakenly thought that the King James version
was the original Bible; they have studied that as the authority
and have thought of other translations as really not being the
Bible but the words of man. But the truth is that the Old
Testament was really written in Hebrew and the New Testament in Greek. Many persons have read the Bible as though
it were written directly to themselves. For them it has carried
a meaning which seemed obvious when based on the assumption that it had been written by the author, God, directly to
them. Generally, however, Bible readers do not understand
all the passages they read. Their reading is very selective;
they read passages which meet their needs. According to one
old custom, now seldom practiced, the Bible was opened and
the first passage which met the eye gave the answer to the
reader's question.

TODAY'S USE OF THE BIBLE.—Many may want to get
help from the Bible, yet cannot. They may be like the student
who said to her Bible instructor, "My grandmother read the
Bible a lot, but she never taught my mother anything about it.
And now she's dead and I cannot ask her. I quit going to the
church I was attending because my minister did not answer
my questions and kept putting me off. He insisted in taking

everything literally, and I could not believe it that way. Geology tells us the world is millions of years old. The only way I could take it was that each day was a million years. I took this course because I wanted to learn about the Bible. My mother also wanted me to. There is a sort of empty feeling and I wouldn't want my children to grow up with that. It isn't that I am not religious. I know there is a God who caused all the things in the world, but I can't believe what I was taught about the Bible in the light of what I learned in school."

As she took the course she discovered that in the last two generations much new light had been shed on the Bible. Manuscripts have been found which are older and more nearly like the original copies. Studies have been made of many of the books so that we now know much more about how they came to be written. Archeologists have uncovered the ruins of whole cities, and these discoveries have helped us to understand better the people to whom the words were first written. Men who have spent a lifetime at study have made translations in an attempt to express in better English the very oldest available manuscripts of the Biblical books.

TODAY'S INDIFFERENCE TOWARD THE BIBLE.—The observer does not need to be very keen eyed to see that the student of a few paragraphs back is not alone. The Bible has gone from the parlor table and Bible reading from the daily schedule. Maybe it isn't all a lack of interest; people are often perplexed when they read a passage that cannot be explained scientifically. After all, science is the authority nowadays. Also, many passages in the Bible seem to have no application to our day, which has so rapidly become different. Until the beginning of the nineteenth century, living conditions were not very different from those of Biblical times. The Bible deals with the life of the shepherd, the farmer, and the small business man; it does not deal with the life of the airplane pilot, the manager of large industry, or the international banker. Another reason may be the fact that people are so busy doing things that they do not find time for reading and thinking. Yet there is an eager desire to recapture what the Bible meant to former generations.

A NEW APPROACH NEEDED.—A new approach to the Bible often attends a religious revival or a new religious movement. That was true of the beginnings of Christianity, of the work of the Protestant reformers, and of the Evangelical movement that was led by the Wesleys and Whitefield in England in the eighteenth century. In our own day, new patterns of thought can be adapted to the needs of man.

The Bible may be studied as the revelation of God, unfolding a little at a time [14] until it was completed in Jesus. Jesus seems to have expected the unfolding to continue.[15] The individual may learn in the same way the human race learned—by a planned reading of the Bible. He can achieve this by studying the persons who wrote the words and the first readers, the purpose for writing the book, and the social and religious conditions existing at the time of writing. He can then study the realistic life situations and concrete experiences of the living persons with whom the book began. To see how the needs of living persons then were met will help him see how the needs of living persons can be met now.

One should read the Bible for its moral and religious truths. Sometimes the Biblical writer explains an event in terms not in harmony with the explanation which would be made of a similar event in our day. We must recognize that the Bible is not a book on science. That some passages may disagree with modern science ought not to interfere with a person's getting the moral or religious truth from a particular

[14] Hebrews 1:1–4.
[15] John 16:12, 13.

passage. Some persons give to events recorded in the Bible an unscientific explanation, when such an explanation is wholly unnecessary. There is the church school teacher who was telling the story of Peter sleeping on the roof of the house of Simon the tanner. An alert youngster, looking through the window at the sloping roof of the house next door, asked how Peter could lie on the roof asleep without rolling off. She could have explained that the roofs of the Palestinian houses were flat and that the people often slept on the roofs. Instead she said, "Well, you know that with God all things are possible." Such explanations of minor matters often so repel people that they fail to get the essential moral or religious teaching.

One should look to the Bible for the moral tone of modern religious living rather than for an authoritative set of rules. For example, one need not accept St. Paul as an authority for the hair-do of the girls of the twentieth century.[16]

The use of the Bible should be selective. That is the way our grandmothers read it. The Gospel of John was a favorite gospel, but only portions of it were read often: John 3:16 and the fourteenth chapter. Many types of thought and behavior found in the Bible have no counterpart in modern life. In numerous other cases one can abstract the values and apply them to modern situations. Many Scriptural passages are suited to the devotional needs of the twentieth century Christian, as, for example, Psalm 100. Other passages give a sense of security or a sense of direction. Still others suggest valuable help in practical living. If, for example, the reader seeks the answer to the question of the Christian attitude toward race prejudice, he may read about Peter's dream about ceremonially unclean food [17] or Jesus' parable of the good Samaritan.[18] In order to read selectively, it is important

[16] I Corinthians 11:13–16; I Peter 3:3.
[17] Acts 10.
[18] Luke 10:30–37.

first to read the Bible rather more widely and note the passages which promise to be of help. As this calls for regular Bible reading and study, the first matter we will discuss is how to read the Bible to learn what is in it.

SUGGESTIONS FOR BIBLE READING.—We would suggest that you read one book all the way through. For this we would recommend Matthew, unless you think that is too large for a start. James or First Thessalonians could be alternatives. As you read, make notes on a piece of paper with the chapter and verse. Or you might get a dollar edition of the American Standard Version which you can underline, and make notes in the margin. You would note: (1) what helps you, (2) questions you want answered, and (3) what it tells you about the author and the first readers of the book. Next, read about the book in a good Bible commentary. After you have read what the commentary has to say, read the book again, if possible in one or two sittings. Then outline the book. In this way you will come to know what is really in the Bible.

Now if you think this is too laborious, consider this simpler way. Just read the book through, and after reading each chapter write down in about fifty words the substance of the chapter. After finishing the book, read all your notes through at one time to get a complete picture of the book.

Of course, the first thing is to get a knowledge of what the Bible contains. Once you have done that, you are ready to get help from it. After you have finished one book, you are ready to get help from that book.

Now let us see how you can be helped. Suppose someone has wronged you. It may be only a slight offense, or it may be someone has done you harm, hurt your reputation, or prevented you from getting some cherished object. You really want to know what is the Christian attitude toward that person. Your reading has taught you that in Romans 12 there is something about that. You turn to Romans 12 and read, "Avenge not yourselves, but rather give place unto wrath: for it is written, Vengeance is mine; I will repay, saith the Lord. Therefore if thine enemy hunger, feed him; if he thirst, give him drink: for in so doing thou shalt heap coals of fire on his head. Be not overcome of evil, but overcome evil with good." [19]

You know also that Jesus said something that ought to help you, according to Matthew 5, and you turn to the 44th verse and read, "Love your enemies, bless them that curse you, do good to them that hate you, and pray for them which despitefully use you, and persecute you; That ye may be the children of your Father which is in heaven: for he maketh his sun to rise on the evil and on the good, and sendeth rain on the just and on the unjust."

Now those verses haven't told you just what to do to John Smith, but they have told you enough to make it clear that whatever you do to John, it should be to do him good and not merely to express your anger and resentment.

But suppose you did not know about these passages. Then the only thing for you to do is to read until you have found something that will help you.

But sometimes you will want to read just for inspiration or as a means of worship. This would be a good time to read again those passages which inspired you when you first read them. One can never forget his first reading of the seventeenth chapter of John. What a thrill to think of Jesus back there nineteen hundred years ago, praying for you, an American in the twentieth century! And the First Psalm. The present writer copied it down in his notebook of the best literature, and later memorized it. There are many other such passages you will cherish very dearly.

[19] Romans 12:19–21.

FOR DISCUSSION

1. Which comes first chronologically, the words of the Law or the words of the Prophets?
2. Make lists of the books of the Old Testament included in the Law, those in the Prophets, and those in the Writings.
3. Make a brief outline of the history of the Bible.
4. Make a list of the translations of the Bible into English and the dates.
5. Could we say that Jesus was "a Man of the Book"? Give evidence for your answer.
6. Contrast the use of the Bible by the early church with that of the early Protestants.
7. Should a person interpret each passage of the Bible as though it has been written directly to him? Give reasons for your answer.
8. Talk to a number of your fellow students to find out whether or not they read the Bible regularly, and why or why not.
9. Compare the way you have adopted for reading the Bible with that described in this chapter. How does some one of your acquaintances go about getting help from the Bible?

CHAPTER 2

What Is the Christian's Idea of God?

> My one unchanged obsession
> Wherever my feet have trod
> Is a keen enormous haunting
> Never-sated thirst for God.
>
> GAMALIEL BRADFORD *

When discussing religion, which to most of us means Christianity, the first thought often is about God. People have different ideas of God, just as children have different ideas of their parents or of their friends. So it happens that Christians think differently about God. The co-author of this book, for example, likes to speak of the Holy Ghost. The writer of this chapter prefers the Holy Spirit.

Names express thoughts, and different terms are used to express different ideas about the same thing. God was called by various names to convey differing conceptions of Him. The prophets of the Old Testament often indicated their ideas of God by the terms they used in writing about Him; Jesus used the same terms but gave them a different emphasis; and since His day Christians have continued to finds ways to express their thoughts of God.

A. Faith in God

Christians all over the world begin their prayers with the words, "Our Father who art in heaven." They are found in the prayer which Jesus taught His disciples. This is something more than a convenient way to address God in prayer. The idea of the fatherhood of God was highly emphasized by Jesus' teaching and His life.

* Quoted from *Shadow Verses,* copyright 1920, by permission of Yale University Press.

18

THE PROPHET'S IDEA OF GOD.—Jesus inherited the thought of God as a father from the religious teachers of his nation. Since the nation seemed more important than the individual, Hosea thought of God as the father of the nation rather than as the father of individuals.[1] The fatherly love of God was expressed in tender solicitous terms. The Psalmist had a more intimate and personal belief, and thought that God looked upon each person as His child.[2] The use of "father" among other titles in the prayer of Ben-Sirach indicates also a personal relationship between God and the individual.[3] However, Old Testament writers hardly ever spoke of God as father. They thought of Him as a king and a judge. He was just,[4] loving,[5] and holy,[6] and the Creator of the ends of the earth.[7]

JESUS' IDEA OF GOD.—On the other hand, Jesus favored the idea of the fatherhood of God. Any other relationship between God and man was incidental. He compared God to a king,[8] but the likeness was incomplete. He compared God to a judge,[9] but from one point of view only. One should keep in mind that the idea of fatherhood is a potential conception and is very much enriched by Jesus. If one thinks of God as Creator he is reminded that on the will and act of the father depends the origin of his child. God's providence is like that of a father.[10] The yearning love of God is like that of a father who never gives up till the wandering son comes home.[11] Thus the highest type of earthly father becomes the symbol of God. Indeed, we are reminded that God's goodness is greater than that of the human father.[12]

[1] Hosea 11:1.
[2] Psalms 103:13.
[3] Ecclesiasticus 23:1, 4 (Apocrypha).
[4] Amos 5:24.
[5] Hosea 11:1.
[6] Isaiah 6:3.
[7] Isaiah 40:28.
[8] Matthew 22:2-13.
[9] Luke 18:1-8.
[10] Matthew 7:9.
[11] Luke 15:12-32.
[12] Matthew 7:11.

We Americans of the twentieth century must keep in mind that the place of father changes with the changing times and scenes. If we think that Jesus considered God in the category with the "old man," we are greatly mistaken. Anyone who thinks of dad as the man who goodnaturedly or otherwise struggles to pay the bills and so has little time to enter into the family life must revise his ideas about God as Father.

One should, perhaps, think of the father as the benevolent dictator in the home. The apostle Paul got his ideas of the father's place from his own Jewish home life. He urged wives to be subject to their husbands in everything, and urged children to obey their parents. The man was limited by his devotion to his wife and by a care not to provoke his children to wrath.[13]

Jesus seems to have thought that the ideal for the human race was the very best type of home. Probably He thought in terms of His own at Nazareth, where the family ties were very close.[14] This close relationship continued after Jesus left the home to take up His traveling ministry of teaching.[15] Jesus enlarged that relationship to include all who do God's will.[16]

We may be sure that Jesus included those who did not belong to His own religious and racial group. He not only quoted with approval but made central in His teaching the Scriptural formula, "Thou shalt love thy neighbor as thyself."[17] The first line of the couplet which definitely restricted this love to the Israelite nation He did not quote.[18] All men might look to God as their Father.[19]

Not only does Jesus teach that God is the Father, but He also urged His followers to live as children of God should. He said that they should love their enemies that they might

[13] Ephesians 5:24, 25; 6:1, 4. See also I Timothy 3:4.
[14] Luke 2:51.
[15] Matthew 12:46, 47.
[16] Matthew 12:50.
[17] Matthew 19:19.
[18] Leviticus 19:18.
[19] Matthew 8:11; 5:43–48.

become the "children of your Father which is in heaven ..." [20]
He assumed that a son would ethically be like his father. His
own relationship to God was revealed in His ethical likeness to
God.[21] His enemies were like their "father, the devil." [22]
Ethical likeness to God implies divine sonship.[23]

No analogy is complete enough wholly to contain a person's
ideas about God. Jesus does not cast all His thoughts about
God in the mold of fatherhood. He shared the conception
of the prophets. He believes in the holiness of God.[24] God
is righteous and just. He loves man with a yearning and
intense devotion even to the faithless and unworthy.[25] Jesus
assumes that God is the creator,[26] that God controls nature,
and that His gifts are for all.[27] Jesus trusts in God's care.[28]

THE NEW TESTAMENT VIEW OF GOD.—The New Testa-
ment writers were largely influenced by the thinking of Jesus.
Paul sometimes follows the teaching of the rabbis. The writer
of the letter to the Hebrews does not speak of God as the
father. Other exceptions may be noted but, by and large, the
idea of God held by Jesus dominates the view of the early
Christians.

In brief summary, we find New Testament Christians
accepting certain ideas of God found in the Old Testament.
He is loving, just, and holy. He created the heavens and the
earth and all that is in them. To these concepts have been
added three distinctive New Testament ideas of God. (1) He
is the father of all mankind and so all men are brothers.
(2) He is the Father of Jesus Christ, and that relationship is
revealed in Jesus' ethical likeness to God. (3) The self-
sacrificing love of God was made manifest in the life and
death of Christ.

[20] Matthew 5:44–45.
[21] John 10:36–37.
[22] John 8:44.
[23] Matthew 7:21.
[24] Matthew 6:9.
[25] Luke 15; Mark 8:31–33.
[26] Mark 10:6.
[27] Matthew 5:45.
[28] Luke 12:24–32; Matthew 6:26–34.

WHAT WE THINK OF GOD TODAY.—Sometimes Christians say that God is all-wise, or omniscient, although many do not stop to consider all that these words mean. For instance, does God know all that will happen in the future? He knows so much more than we do that it would be impossible for us to suggest all that is in His mind. Most would agree that if one is to have faith in God he must believe that He knows what is best. This is the kind of God the Bible and Christian theology describe.

Not only do we think of God as wiser than man, but we recognize that He is better than man. He is holy, that is, morally perfect. The pagans could sometimes complain of their gods that they did what their best men would not do. That could never be said of the Christian's God. On the contrary, He is held up as the moral goal of mankind.[29]

If we are to have faith in God, we must know that He has good intentions. Christianity furnishes the basis for this faith. The Christian God is righteous. Now righteousness implies both goodness and justice. We think of justice in terms of people getting what is coming to them—both rewards and punishments. Not only does God have good intentions, but He is trustworthy. We can depend on Him to do what is right.

Sometimes it is difficult to harmonize the characteristics of God. Justice—in the sense of meting out punishment—and love are difficult to reconcile. The present writer was a counselor in a young people's camp a few years ago. One of the young ladies, who at that time was twenty-four years old and happily married, related an incident about her sister. The two girls had been orphaned when they were quite young. The one was brought up in a Christian home where through her home and church relations she had enjoyed a satisfying religious experience. Her sister, on the contrary, was brought

[29] Matthew 5:48.

up in a home where there were no religious observances or church connections. In young womanhood the sister had died without ever having made any profession of religious faith.

When she had related the incident she asked, "Do you think my sister is lost?" Her question meant, "Do you think she failed to get to heaven?" In answering her query the New Testament view of God as stated by John was used as a basis; "God is love." [30] Her question was answered with another, "Would you condemn her to everlasting punishment?" Of course she said "No," and then it was we reasoned, "You must remember that God loves your sister more than you do."

This attitude is true to the Christian conception of God. However, a person must not take advantage of God's love and mercy in such way as to be careless about right and wrong. God is also just. An emphasis upon His justice would help us all to live better lives.

B. God in Nature

Christians believe that God is more than nature. By nature we mean the material universe. Nevertheless they do not believe that it is independent of Him. He reveals Himself through nature. The fullness of the whole earth is His glory. (This is a literal translation of Isaiah 6:3.) Bishop Berkeley spoke of nature as a divine language. God is the creator of the nature which reveals Him. He made all that was made. He is present in all His works.

Today we think of nature more from the point of view of the natural sciences than of religion. Since we study natural laws instead of nature's revelation of God, it would be well to approach the place of God in nature from the point of view of His relation to natural laws.

The summer breeze blows against one's face, covered with perspiration, and brings a cooling sensation and relief from

[30] I John 4:16.

the heat, and we can turn to God gratefully for the benefit brought by the breeze. Stronger currents of air bring rain clouds which water the growing crops; but one must see that the same order of events brings a roaring tornado which we do not view with any gratefulness to an overshadowing providence. It would be very difficult, however, for us to say that a different power was responsible for the air currents in the case of the cooling summer breeze. The sun in the springtime gives to the ground warmth which awakens life in the dormant plants and seed. An increasing amount of heat from the same sun sometimes burns up the crops. It would be difficult to say that a loving and wise providence provided the warmth of the springtime and did not bring the burning heat of the drought.

Scientists, however, have discovered an orderliness in these seemingly contradictory processes. They have spoken of it as the uniformity of nature. It is the principle which makes it possible for us to count on certain events following certain others, or, as we say, effects follow causes. This uniformity of nature, this orderliness, makes it possible, for example, for doctors to formulate treatment for certain ailments and to apply those treatments to persons who have those ailments. Nature's laws are immutable and therefore the universe is dependable and trustworthy.

In the light of these considerations God seems to present us a universe in which we can feel a sense of security. Without that sense of security this world would be an unpleasant place in which to live—and that is an understatement. If natural processes were not orderly what kind of madhouse would we be living in? It would be a place in which thinking would be impossible. As we look at the natural order, we are assured that orderly processes work for the good of man. It is the exceptional case in which these orderly processes bring harm to man.

But these exceptions come often enough and are serious enough to disturb many persons. Some Christians· suggest the possibility of miracles to take care of such special situations. We are accustomed to making exceptions in our man-made rules and regulations when they prove unfair to a given individual. So they ask, might not God set aside the order of nature in these exceptional cases?

Others, however, sharply react against belief in miracles because, as a professor of education once said, "I have too much faith in science." Miracles have become something to explain. Once upon a time people believed in Christianity because of the miracles. Today it is more likely that one accepts the miracles because of his belief in Christianity.

Before coming to the conclusion that exceptions should be made in the operation of natural laws, let us consider what would happen in these special situations. Suppose that a man in despair decides to take his own life and jumps from the top of a cliff. On the way down he may hastily repent of his impulsive action. Why, then, should he not be saved from crashing at the bottom of the cliff? To save him within the order of nature God would have to allow all the people on the earth to fly from the face of the earth.

Natural order, God's orderly way of doing things, then becomes a means of fixing responsibility for human action upon human beings. If exceptions were made in the natural processes, what irresponsibile persons human beings would become! If God guided a bullet to the heart of a grizzly bear attacking a hunter, and deflected the bullet from the heart of a murderer's victim, what clowns we would become! We would be like children playing at cops and robbers, pulling the triggers of imaginary weapons at other children behind a hedge.

We do read in the New Testament, of course, of Jesus' miracles and of the miracles of Peter and Paul and the others.

Some scholars classify the miracles as healing miracles, nature miracles, etc. They believe that Jesus and his followers treated the patients according to certain spiritual laws which we are just now beginning to learn and put into practice in psychosomatic medicine. Jesus did often express forgiveness before the physical healing. C. G. Jung, the eminent Swiss psychiatrist, and others have noticed that a physical pathological condition has been relieved after confession of certain painful psychological facts. Of course, faith is an element in healing. We shall study this later in the study of prayer. Some persons are convinced that the miracles were performed in harmony with natural laws not understood at the time.

However that may be, it is the Christian belief that God created the world, that He is working in it and through it, and that He is revealed by it. Many are inspired by the wonder and beauty of nature to think of God. Many others are impressed with the thought that God is a great mathematician, or a great artisan, as they study scientifically the facts about this universe.

C. God in Christ

Christians believe that Jesus is the Son of God. This means different things to different people. Most Christians think that this belief depends upon the doctrine of the Virgin birth.[31] To Christians through the centuries this unique origin of the physical body of Jesus has indicated His unique relationship to God. To those who have thought more deeply, the doctrine of the Virgin birth becomes the explanation of the doctrine of the incarnation. They believe that God lived in human form. This doctrine involves them in difficulties. Some of these difficulties are represented by these questions: How can we believe that God is the changeless and eternal

[31] Matthew 1:18–25.

one if He took on the form and limitations of humanity? How can we explain the experience of close fellowship of Jesus with God in prayer? Did He call Himself "Father"? In spite of these difficulties, they believe that the Christian faith is that the Eternal God shared the experiences of humanity. This explains the way the grace of God becomes a gift to man.

Others explain the sonship of Jesus as consisting in ethical likeness.[32] The early disciples of Jesus were so impressed with the thought that Christ was like God that they called Him by the names they used in speaking of God.[33]

We cannot get a very clear picture of God apart from Christ, but immediately when we say that God is like Christ we can learn what God is like. Let us see what Christ is like. As we read the Gospel story about the healing of the paralytic we learn that it is not the will of God that anyone should be paralyzed. We learn about the yearning love of God for the wanderer in the touching story of the prodigal son.[34] Thus we are taught that God rejoices when His sons come home, no matter how sinful they have been. But He does not wait for them to come home. He goes out and seeks them as the shepherd sought his lost sheep.[35] Christ sealed that story with Calvary, and when His heart broke on Calvary He expressed the measure of God's love for a world of sinners. Truly He is the Son of God.

The thought that Jesus is proclaimed the Son of God through His death and resurrection is expressed in the words of Paul to the Romans.[36] Notice the emphasis upon the words "with power." The Son of God had lived upon the earth in weakness and humility.[37] Paul believed that Christ had been glorified and had received great power at the resurrection.[38]

[32] John 10:36-37; Matthew 5:44-46.
[33] Acts 2:36.
[34] Luke 15:12-32.
[35] Luke 15:4-10.
[36] Romans 1:4.
[37] Romans 8:3.
[38] Philippians 2:9-11.

Thus we have seen that in Christian thinking God was in Christ or was revealed through Christ in His birth, in His life, in His death and resurrection. A great many times Christians have become involved in discussion of biological facts or metaphysical theories and have overlooked the essential truth. The various doctrines and points of view which we have discussed in this section are all ways of expressing the unique truth that God somehow participated in the life of Jesus as in that of no other being. A modern Christian put it in this way, that in Christ was all of God there could be in a human life. Through all the Christian centuries the followers of Jesus have always thought of Him as the highest they knew. Christians have always turned to Christ when they wanted to find God.

D. God in Human Life

An idea came like a bolt out of the blue to a student of theology as he sat in a prayer meeting. The idea was that just as Jesus had revealed God, so Christians should reveal Jesus. The theology student was not the first one to have that idea. In another form it was the theme of Jesus' prayer for His disciples.[39]

CONTINUATION OF JESUS' WORK.—In Christian thinking and living there is a divine fellowship. The need of that fellowship was sensed in the very beginning by John, as a means of continuing the work of Jesus. Jesus' body would be gone, but His followers would still feel His presence.[40] And so it has been; Jesus is present with those who follow his teachings.[41] The presence of Jesus seems to be of a spiritual nature. In fact, he who comes to take the place of Jesus in the flesh is usually called the Holy Spirit.[42] Through the Spirit, the revelation of God does and will continue.[43]

[39] John 17:21.   [41] John 14:22 f.   [43] John 16:12-13.
[40] John 14:18 f.   [42] John 14:25-26.

We get the conception of the divine fellowship as a continuation of the work of Jesus in the story of the day of Pentecost. In the experience which followed on the day of Pentecost, the disciples said that they had received the gift of the Holy Spirit.[44] What was the gift of the Holy Spirit? In order to answer that question let us go back into the religious experience of the disciples.

As Jesus and his disciples lived together, the great stores of truth in Jesus' teachings enlightened them. They also discovered it was easier to do things they knew they should do when they were with Him, just as we discover it easier to do right with some persons than it is with others.

This is the reason why they were so lost after the crucifixion that they went back to their fishing and gave up the noble ideals which they had learned from Jesus. It is true that He returned to them after three days, but they did not realize the helpfulness of the old fellowship. Sometimes He came to them through a closed door, or again He appeared unexpectedly to them at their daily duties. They never could be sure when He was near, and in His presence was power.

After ten days of this kind of uncertain experience they became aware of a great incoming of spiritual power. They believed that it was Jesus who had poured out this spirit in them.[45] The power and the courage which they felt in the days of Jesus' earthly life they now felt again. It was an even greater inspiration and they now went out on their own to the great work of preparing people for the kingdom of God.

Later other Christians said that God (or Christ) dwelt in them.[46] How can one person dwell in another? As one becomes like the other. Have you ever heard anyone say, "As long as you live your mother won't die?" What did he mean?

[44] Acts 2:4; 10:45. [45] Acts 2:33.
[46] II Corinthians 6:16; Ephesians 3:6; I John 4:15.

Why, he simply meant that the child is so much like the mother that her likeness will live in the child. So the likeness of God lives in us if His Holy Spirit dwells in us.

Christians down through the centuries have received the gift of the Holy Spirit and have felt the indwelling of the Holy Spirit. Some think of this as a second work of grace occurring after conversion. It is a cleansing (sanctifying) and empowering experience. Others feel the inspiration and power of the Holy Spirit in their lives from the day of conversion or confirmation, or from some time so early that they cannot remember when it began.

The spirit of God dwelling in man means a great deal to a person. On the day of Pentecost the disciples first realized that Jesus had come to live in their hearts. This revelation gave them courage. The apostle Peter was sometimes very timid, as when he denied Christ three times at the trial. After he had received the gift of the Holy Spirit he became a courageous crusader.[47] Many others have had the same inspiriting experience.

The gift of the Holy Spirit means increased power. In this connection, consider the conversation of a student with a former teacher about what a person gets out of conversion. The teacher said that a drunkard who decided to join the church would find, when in the presence of the temptation to drink, that he was just about as weak as he had been the day before conversion. Let us grant that a drunkard will have to put up a hard fight to overcome the temptation but, so far as his power is concerned, there is all the difference in the world. Before he turned to God for help he was only a weak human being struggling against fearful odds, but when he asks God's help he calls upon the One who moves the stars in their courses. He has all the power of the universe subject to his call.

[47] Acts 4:8–13.

The gift of the Holy Spirit means a closer fellowship.[48] The fellowship is a fellowship among Christians and between Christians and God.[49] This fellowship was promoted in the early church by the agape, or love feast. Jesus promised to be with Christians wherever they were gathered together. This fellowship was also expressed by Paul as, time after time, he indicated that the Church was the body of Christ.[50]

Another figure that was used often by Paul was "the temple of the Holy Spirit." [51] He thought that God was dwelling in the Christian so that the body became His temple, His dwelling place. As we think of God in human life, we think of the revelation of God through human beings and in human living. We think also of God as a source of power in human living.

Christians have always believed in some form of this three-fold revelation of God. This is the doctrine of the Trinity. God is the Father, the maker of heaven and earth and all that is in them. God is the Son, as we understand Him, in the life and death of Jesus Christ. God is the Holy Spirit as He lives in the heart of man and gives him inspiration and courage.

For Discussion

1. Describe various ways in which God is like an earthly father. Also the ways in which Christians are like children in their relation to God.

2. Are there respects in which God is not like earthly fathers? Did Jesus point them out?

3. Do you think that Jesus is ethically like God? What do you think of ethical likeness as an indication of kinship?

4. Are there evidences that God does not control nature? Was Jesus right in trusting God when Jesus finally was crucified?

[48] Acts 2:42.
[49] Matthew 18:20.
[50] I Corinthians 12:27.
[51] I Corinthians 6:19.

5. Do you have trouble believing that God is both in nature and above nature? Try to think of some illustration of a man being in something, yet more than the thing.

6. What characteristics of God enable us to trust "where we cannot see"?

7. In modern times, Christians have emphasized the love of God. Think of reasons why His justice should be emphasized also.

8. What would you say to a person who exclaims, "I don't see how one can believe in a good God when war and famine and suffering are in the world"?

9. Write for yourself all the various ways that Christ is related to God.

10. Think of your own life and ask what people think of Christ if they believe your life to be a revelation of Him.

11. Does the presence of human beings strengthen and inspire us? Is this anything like the power and inspiration which come from the presence of God?

CHAPTER 3

What Is Man?

HAIL MAN!

This flesh is but the symbol and the shrine
Of an immense and unimagined beauty,
Not mortal, but divine;
Structure behind our structure,
Lightning within the brain,
Soul of the singing nerve and throbbing vein,
A giant blaze that scorches through our dust,
Fanning our futile "might be" with its "must";
Bearing upon its breast our eager span—
Beyond, above and yet the self of man!

ANGELA MORGAN *

A. The Origin of Man

The most remarkable statement in the creation story [1] is in the very first verse of Genesis, "In the beginning *God*." *God* created man and all things living and inanimate.

Scientists try to tell us just how God did this. Since the Bible is not a textbook on Anthropology, Geology, Astronomy, or any other science, it does not attempt to tell us exactly how God performed the act of creation or how long it took Him to do it. The Bible is the textbook of the Christian Religion and presents man in a religious light. The Bible emphasizes the dignity of man as a child of God, capable of living in fellowship with Him. We see God as the creative force in all nature, not the abstract force of pantheism but a personal force in creation. The Bible tells us about what

* Quoted by permission of the author.
[1] Genesis 1:1-31.

was created by God and covers the scene well. The story could not have been better written because nothing is omitted. It is the task of science to tell us just how it was done and to reveal the laws of nature by which we live here.

THE CREATION STORY AND SCIENCE.—The Genesis account tells us that God formed man of the dust of the earth.[2] If the body is buried in the ground and remains there long enough, it returns to the dust from whence it came. We find the same ingredients in the body that are found in the earth.

Then, too, there is a marked resemblance between the body of man and that of some other creatures. As we dissect bodies of animals we find nervous systems, muscles, and internal organs that resemble the human. For that reason it is relatively easy to come to the conclusion that man is an animal pure and simple.

Man also has some reflexes and some reactions in common with some animals. So there are those who come to the conclusion that man's personality is just the sum of his natural responses to physical stimuli. He is a brute the same as any other animal. Occasionally a wife arrives at that conclusion, but she has reference to one man in particular; whereas we are speaking of man in general, and she has "reasons" for her conclusion that we would not want to include in this discussion.

But since man is so often regarded as an animal, we are taught that food, clothing, and shelter are the primary necessities of life. If that be true, the horse has the advantage over man because he can grow his own clothing without conscious effort.

The Christian thinker recognizes with the Bible that man is more than a creature of flesh, blood, and nerves. There is a difference between man and the other creatures, and the Bible

[2] Genesis 2 :7.

tells us why.[3] Before God created man He could look upon all that He had made and not a portion of it could speak to Him, love Him, or have any fellowship with Him. Then He created man in His own image so that man could know Him. When in discussions of the creation of man the question arose, "Why did God do it?" philosophical terms were used to explain the simple fact that God is love and His love must be requited.

Whether God performed this act of creation six thousand or six million years ago makes no difference as far as the "why" of it is concerned. Neither is it so very important if He did it in one master stroke at the beginning, or if it required centuries of development, or if God, at a specific time in the development of His creation, felt the urge to make a creature in His own image and reached down on the sixth day some six thousand years ago and did it.

While man does resemble other living creatures in certain physical aspects, yet there are clear distinctions between him and them. 1. The first distinction readily noticeable is that man walks erect and almost all other creatures use four legs. Some animals may be trained to walk erect on two legs, but the act is unnatural, while it is unnatural for man to walk on four. 2. Man is the only creature who can love. Dog lovers may argue that a dog has a loyalty akin to love and examples of maternal love in some degree are found throughout nature. But the dog's loyalty or love is largely a matter of food and shelter, reflex reactions to outward stimuli. 3. Man has memory, reason, and imagination. With these he can interpret stimuli and direct his reactions. He can plan a course of action far into the future. 4. Man can speak. By means of certain defined sounds produced by the throat and mouth he can interpret his ideas to other men. Animals may to some extent communicate with each other through vocal

[3] Genesis 1:26; 2:7.

sounds, but certainly only meagerly. 5. Man can adapt the things of the earth to his own will. With limitations he can find and develop forces and resources that God has placed at his disposal on the earth. 6. Man appreciates beauty, be it in architecture, nature, painting, sculpture, music, or technique. 7. Man has certain definite hopes for an everlasting life. 8. Man can pray. 9. Man is a moral creature with a conscience. He distinguishes between right and wrong and makes customs, rules, and regulations to govern his life and social relationship.[4]

Man may resemble other creatures in his physical being. But the physical is only a part of man. Those who would regard man only as an animal fail to take his full being into consideration. One of the main drives in human life, ego projection, is little known in the animal world.

These distinctive characteristics set man apart in the creation. The same Almighty hand created other things, but when God's love remained unrequited He made this being in His own image. In man He made one who could talk with Him, love Him, and have fellowship with Him.[5]

To summarize the thoughts on the origin of man it may be said that God created him on a higher plane than the other creatures,[6] endowed him with unique intellectual and spiritual gifts, and gave him dominion over the earth. He has physical characteristics in common with other creatures, but the physical is only a part of his nature. How long it took God to make man or just when He did it is of minor consequence. The important thing is that God made man.

B. The Nature of Man

Now that we have briefly discussed the origin of man and see that he is more than a physical being, it remains for us to explore his nature.

[4] Genesis 3:6.   [5] I John 1:3; Philippians 3:10.   [6] Psalms 8:5, 6.

THE TOTAL PERSONALITY.—Among superstitious people there are those who believe that when a person dies a window should be opened in the room so the soul can make its exit unhampered. It is true that there is something very real about the soul of man, yet it is entirely intangible. Once it leaves the body there is death, and yet we cannot define exactly what the soul is. We know it is a part of the total personality of the human, it is the eternal part of man, the spark of divinity [7] that God gives him. Man cannot be man without it. He can lose portions of his body and still retain his identity, but once his soul is parted from the body what remains is totally devoid of personality.

Man is composed of body, soul, and mind. Reason, imagination, memory, the ability to perceive stimuli and respond to them, the capacity for love or worship, and the inclination to catch a cold are all a part of his nature. The inner experience of the presence of God and the consciousness that his being is eternal are also a part of him.

In estimating the nature of man, all factors of his being must be considered. Human natures differ in that there are variations of these factors and each of these phases of the personality is also composed of many interrelated portions. We know that each person differs in some degree from all others in physical appearance. There is also a wide variation in his mental and spiritual make-up. This variation and interrelationship bring into being the various types of personality found among us. In dealing with persons there can be no hard and fast rules because each one is a unique being. This applies in all human relationships. When a leader wants to get mass action of any sort he will achieve his aim only in so far as he is able to mold personalities into a kind of class on the basis of some motives or ideals common to the group.

[7] Genesis 2:7.

In the ministry of healing we are aware of the fact that the various phases of the personality have something to do with it. Neither can one phase be treated entirely apart from the others. Jesus recognized that also,[8] and took the intellectual and spiritual into consideration when He performed miracles of healing.[9]

The element of faith in healing is recognized by the Lord, as well as the stress of guilt.[10] When the man with the palsy realized that his sins were forgiven and he was at ease in this respect, then our Lord proceeded to heal his physical illness.

How Man Became Conscious of His Personality.— In the Old Testament man is considered as a social being and his value is calculated on the basis of his identity with a group. The group with which he had his first contact was that of the family or clan. The wrong of one member was a wrong of all the members; a disgrace upon one, a disgrace upon all. Likewise if a harm was done to one member of the family, the others felt it their duty to avenge that wrong.[11] And that vengeance was not necessarily directed solely against the person who did the wrong, but rather against the whole family or clan. All should feel the brunt of a wrong done by one of the members. In the days of David,[12] when a famine came over the land it was blamed on Saul's slaughter of the Gibeonites. To make atonement David asked the Gibeonites what justice they wanted and they asked for the lives of seven of Saul's sons. Instead, two sons and five grandsons were slain. It didn't make any difference since all were considered guilty. In our opinion they were entirely innocent, but in those days an individual was so closely identified with the group that Saul's sons could make restitution in his stead.

[8] Matthew 8:3–4.
[9] Matthew 9:28–30; Mark 2:5; Luke 6:8–10.
[10] Mark 9:23, 24; Luke 5:20–24.
[11] Genesis 14:14–16.
[12] II Samuel 21:1–14.

Another instance is that of Ahab and Jezebel.[13] After these two unjustly condemned Naboth to death and confiscated his property, Jehu led a successful revolt against the king. In meting out punishment, he caused not only Ahab and Jezebel to be killed but their sons also because they were considered as being blood guilty with their parents.

In this early period the members were so intimately identified with the group that the group owned the individual. The family or clan held the rights of life and death as far as its members were concerned. The patriarch was the ruler of the clan and could do with the members according to his will. And all the members were responsible for the patriarch's actions. Even the children had no rights of their own.[14] Jephthah could make a vow to devote to the Lord whatever came forth from the door of his house. When it turned out to be his daughter, she had no rights in the matter.

As the economic and social life changed, so did the conception of man. As towns and cities arose, tribal solidarity grew weaker and each member of society emerged as an individual with rights and responsibilities of his own. Individual property rights came into being, and individual moral responsibilities developed. Whereas in former times it was commendable for the individual to merge himself with the group, now it became a virtue for an individual to stand out from the group. Leaders called upon each one to make a decision.[15] Personal religious loyalty to God or to principles became praiseworthy and the group was left behind by those higher-minded persons who emerged as leaders.

By the time Jesus came upon the scene, society had advanced so far that He could lay emphasis upon the individual. Religion became an intimate personal relationship

---

[13] II Kings 9:24–26; 10:1–11.   [15] I Kings 18:21.
[14] Judges 11:30–40.

with God.[16] Repentance and moral choice became matters for the individual. Salvation was no longer conditioned upon the attitude of the group, but each person was made responsible for his own spiritual welfare as well as his own actions.[17]

MAN AS AN INDIVIDUAL.—Jesus emphasized the importance of the family as a social unit, but each of its members had certain rights and responsibilities.[18] No matter how large the family, each person had certain rights that the group could not assume. Each person was regarded as a child of God or a potential child of God.

God became personal also, rather than tribal. "He that watcheth over Israel" became "He that careth for you." Jesus revealed God to us in His own life. So personal was His feeling toward individuals that even little children were not excluded.[19] He called His disciples one by one rather than by an appeal to a family or a group.[20] He told the parable of the woman who lost one coin [21] and told how God rejoices over one repentant sinner. In the parable of the lost sheep,[22] He said that there is joy in all heaven over one lost sheep when it is found. The individual emerged from the group and became a personality so important that God is interested in his welfare.

This viewpoint does not limit God's love. It is not so individualistic that the welfare of the group or society is overlooked. The parable of the leaven [23] may be applied individually and corporately. The Kingdom of God is personal in that it is the relationship between you and God; it is also social in so far as it leavens society and its principles are applied to human relationships. Jesus could say "the king-

[16] Matthew 6:30.
[17] Luke 15:18; John 8:11.
[18] Matthew 5:31, 32.
[19] Matthew 18:2; Mark 10:14.
[20] John 1:35–50.
[21] Luke 15:8–10.
[22] Luke 15:4–7.
[23] Luke 13:20–21.

dom is within you" [24] and teach His disciples to pray "Thy kingdom come." [25] The one is personal, the other corporate. Those in whose hearts the kingdom is a reality will certainly work to bring the same satisfaction to others. As this kingdom spreads, it will influence relationships and take on a national and international character.[26]

God's interest in the individual's eternal life was also revealed by Jesus. Promises of eternal life were made by Him [27] to those who believe. God's plan for the individual soul reaches out beyond the span of years that he will live in this world. There is another, an eternal world in which the soul will be housed in "a building of God, an house not made with hands, eternal in the heavens." [28]

The New Testament recognizes the importance of the individual person. It brings hope of a rebirth, a new man, a regeneration through faith in Jesus. It regards human nature as potential. It can become good or bad. Sinful people may be reborn. The Holy Spirit may permeate a believer's soul until he becomes inclined toward the good rather than the evil. Jesus and His disciples knew how fickle, hateful, and selfish people can be. But they were convinced that sinful people could also know God and become new beings in Him. It may be said, then, that the important thing as far as human nature is concerned is its possibilities.

C. Man and Suffering

One of the great problems that has always baffled man is the explanation of suffering in God's creation. The question that naturally arises is: "If God is good, why does He permit pain, suffering, and anguish in the world?" Another question often asked is, "Why are the innocent

[24] Luke 17:21.
[25] Matthew 6:10.
[26] Mark 4:30–32.

[27] John 3:15.
[28] II Corinthians 5:1.

made to suffer while so many of the guilty apparently
escape?" In this discussion of man and his relation to suffering we want to take these questions into consideration. But
first we want to consider what suffering is and how it can
be used by man.

WHAT IS SUFFERING?—When God created man, apparently physical pain was not meant for him.[29] Had man
remained in his original state of innocence and purity there
probably would have been no suffering, neither would there
have been other people. When he once transgressed the moral
laws, man lost the perfection of his former state and his being
rebelled against the intrusion of corruption. This rebellion is
known as pain or suffering.

It can be said that the strength of paradise is still in the
human personality, therefore the body and the soul rebel
against any force that would destroy them. We can, then,
explain pain and suffering as revulsion against evil and as
protection of the body. It is also true that if there were no
pain we would all have been destroyed long ago. In its
nature, suffering is neither good nor evil. It is unmoral until
man makes it either moral or immoral.

PRIMITIVE IDEAS OF SUFFERING.—Trying to understand
the presence of suffering, primitive peoples like the early
Hebrews placed a responsibility for its origin with the gods.
Helpless in the face of these things, they came to the conclusion that if misfortune or any other kind of evil or suffering came upon a person it was because the gods looked with
disfavor upon something that he had done. If a person pros-
pered and was relatively free from suffering, it must have
been because he did something which was especially pleasing
to the gods.

So it was in those days that man considered himself to be

[29] Genesis 2:15–17.

completely at the mercy of capricious gods. We find an example of this attitude in an incident that occurred when Moses,[30] with his family, was on his way from Jethro's fields to seek the liberation of the Israelites. Quite unexpectedly God met Moses at an inn and left the impression that He was going to kill him. Moses' wife Zipporah, daughter of the priest, Jethro, knew what the trouble was that caused God's anger. After she circumcised her son everything was all right. Unable to understand suffering, they ascribed it to the will of the gods and let it go at that.

SUFFERING AND A DEPENDABLE GOD.—As the people came more and more to appreciate the real character of God, their former idea of Him as a capricious being faded into the background. As for the Hebrew people, they became believers in the one God, Yahweh or Jehovah. But the centralization of all divine powers in the one God still left the problem of suffering as inexplicable as before.

Whereas in the very early days men had believed that their pleasure or pain was the result of pleasing or displeasing a number of gods, now it became a matter of propitiating one God. One thing God loves above all else, moral goodness on the part of man; one thing He hates above all else and that is moral evil or sin. It then was easy to conclude that all suffering is the result of personal sin.

This conclusion is held by many in our day. We often hear those who are suffering ask the question, "What have I done to be punished like this?" One might answer by asking, "Have you brought this upon yourself?" because this attitude is sometimes the result of a guilt stress. But this reply would be too blunt and only deepen the stress. The question does indicate the prevalence of the idea that suffering is always the result of personal sin.

[30] Exodus 4:24–26.

Since in early Biblical times the individual was so closely identified with the family, clan, or tribe, the sin of one could bring calamity upon all: God's disfavor would rest upon the whole group. Moses himself did not like the idea; he thought it was unfair and pleaded with God about it.[31] He did not think the whole congregation should suffer because Korah had sinned. But the idea was prevalent, even down through the prophets, that the whole tribe suffers because of the sins of a few. The second commandment [32] emphasizes the family relationship and that God will punish the children for the sins of the father. Personal sin was not only a personal matter, but a social scourge that could bring suffering upon the whole family or clan, even after the sinner had died. So, when calamities befell the nation and the people suffered through starvation, drought, or pestilence, it was always possible to find enough sins in incorrigible individuals to account for the tribulation.

God became the absolute arbiter in these matters. He, however, changed from the capricious God of the early days to a dependable God. He would not strike down a person without apparent reason; on the other hand when evil or suffering came there was no doubt that it came from God.[33]

When one generalizes, it is comparatively easy to accept the idea that all suffering is the result of personal sin because some sinners can always be found in any group. But this theory causes much distraction and doubt when it is personalized. Why should an innocent grandchild suffer for the sins of a grandfather it may never have seen or known? Suppose such an infant develops a fatal malady and suffers agony before it is mercifully relieved by death. Would it be justice on the part of God thus to punish an innocent one for sin it never knew? We see that the idea of suffering as the

[31] Numbers 16:22.   [33] Amos 3:6.
[32] Exodus 20:5.

result of personal sin will not always bear close scrutiny when
it is related to an individual person.

SUFFERING AS A PUNISHMENT FOR PERSONAL SIN.——
There emerged out of this problem the idea that punishment
comes to the individual for his personal sins. He must suffer
personally, but not his whole family or clan. The prophet
Jeremiah tried to make the old idea fit the individual.[34] It
seems Jeremiah is the first of the prophets to reach this conclusion. Other and later prophets argued the idea [35] and made
it work both ways. A son will not die because of the sins of
his father, but neither would the father die because of the evil
done by a son.

The idea remained that sin causes suffering, but it became
related only to the individual sinner. Job's friends who came
to see him [36] insisted that his terrible condition was the result
of personal sin on his part. (Incidentally, these three friends
show us how we should not make a sick call.[37] For seven days
and nights they sat there shaking their heads in mourning
over his pitiful condition. Must have been encouraging to
the poor soul!) Their accusations caused Job to deny his
responsibility for his suffering. The purpose of this book of
the Bible is to state the common belief and then refute it.
It is a theory being shattered by plain facts. But, while the
book does teach that personal suffering is not always the
result of personal sin, it leaves us still in the dark as far as
answering the "why" of it is concerned.

The Old Testament closes with the problem of suffering
unanswered. Naturally many good people who suffered
questioned God's justice and others, noticing their state,
joined them. But the later prophets, down to and including
Malachi, could only restate the old idea of sin and punishment,
righteousness and favor, although they added that some day

[34] Jeremiah 31:29-30.
[35] Ezekiel 18:20.
[36] Job 8.
[37] Job 2:11-13

the scales would be balanced and the righteous would receive their reward. The hope of a resurrected life had a firm foundation in the conviction that God is just and some day, some time, everything would be made right.

JESUS' IDEA OF SUFFERING.—Suffering was such a difficult problem because no distinction was made among the types of pain. Anything unpleasant was painful, but no attempt was made to distinguish between mental suffering, spiritual pain, and physical suffering. Nevertheless, once the total personality of man is taken into consideration, the "why" of suffering comes more clearly to light. Jesus plainly indicates that mental pain is the result of personal sin.[38] Greed, avarice, selfishness, gluttony will bring mental anguish and are indications of a lack of faith. There is also the pain of the soul caused by a guilt stress that can result from one or a number of causes. Alienation from God through moral evil may cause even physical illness.[39] Despair, hopelessness, a deep sense of being lost forever, and loneliness are sufferings of the soul that may be caused by sin. Physical suffering may also be the result of personal sin; neglect will bring illness. Social diseases are contracted and distributed through promiscuous sex relations that are forbidden in the seventh commandment,[40] and by Jesus also.[41] The results of some sins are passed on from parents to children. There may be a feeling that this is unfortunate, but if the good parents are to influence their children beneficially, then the evil parents do must live after them also. Jesus definitely stated, however, that every calamity cannot be attributed to some wrongdoing on the part of someone.[42]

So it can be said that some suffering and pain are the results of personal sin and some are not. If a storm passes

[38] Matthew 6:24–34.
[39] John 5:14.
[40] Exodus 20:14.
[41] Matthew 5:28.
[42] Luke 13:4–5.

through a certain vicinity and causes anguish to some individuals, those who escape the suffering do not escape because they are more righteous than the others. In fact, righteousness or sin has nothing to do with the matter. On the other hand if a man broods over a secret sin until he has a nervous breakdown, or wilfully neglects his health until his body breaks under the strain, he is reaping the results of personal sin. A young man and his girl friend were riding in his car when it overturned from the highway and both were killed. He had been driving at a terrific rate of speed when the accident happened. The boy's grief-stricken mother said, "Why did God do this to my boy?" God did not do it to her boy, the boy did it to himself by the sin of recklessness. A grieving father and husband stood by the caskets of his wife and little daughter. They had been drowned in the river as they waded in the water near the shore and stepped into a hole. Neither could swim. The father mourned, "Why did God do this to me?" But he should not have blamed God; the mother should have been more careful. God is blamed for a great deal of suffering that is caused by personal sin.

We will agree then that some suffering is the result of personal sin, but certainly not all.

SUFFERING MAY BE CREATIVE.—There are creative possibilities in suffering. Suffering is the expression of sensitivity, or the ability to feel. This is a necessary condition of life and there can be no life without feeling. The higher the form of being, the more sensitive it is. Since man is the acme of the creation, he is more sensitive to pain and pleasure than any other creature. His ability to suffer and experience pleasure are complementary, he cannot have one capacity without the other.

It remains for man to do something with his suffering. When he uses it constructively, his suffering becomes creative.

It may become a discipline for him, it may teach him patience and submission. It served this purpose for Jesus also.[43] A roster of the martyrs to the faith is a list of men and women who used suffering as a creative process through which they made the presence of Christ very real. The New Testament has many references to the creative power of suffering. Those who would be strong must be tested. One does not know his strength until it has been tried. There are some passages in the Old Testament that indicate that suffering may be creative, such as: "refined in the furnace of affliction." [44] Suffering for Christ became an honorable badge. When the early Christians were thrown into prison or otherwise punished they did not question the justice of the visitation but rather gloried in it. Paul said, "I overflow with joy in all our affliction." [45]   It was a disciplinary method that made him more submissive to the will of God and less selfish in his desires. It helped him gain the mastery over self.

Suffering may be creative, also, in that it causes the individual to draw forth his inner resources of fortitude, faith, ingenuity, and perseverance. Some of the greatest characters humanity has produced have used suffering as a ladder to climb to ever nobler achievements.

It can also have opposite effects; there are many who are embittered by suffering. They lay the blame for the pain on God or some other person and become very bitter and vindictive. Those who come in contact with many sufferers in the hospitals soon learn to discern those who can master suffering and those who let it master them.

In answering the question, "Why must the innocent suffer?" we must also ask, "Just whom would you call an innocent person?" With the exception of a newborn child, there is none who is innocent. Those who lean toward

[43] Hebrews 5:8.   [45] II Corinthians 7:4.
[44] Zechariah 13:9.

Calvinistic theology would question if even a newborn babe is innocent.

There are weaknesses to which the flesh is heir and, when one or more of these attack the body, pain will result whether the body be that of an infant or an adult. Suffering in a child can hardly be attributed to any personal sin until the child is old enough to be responsible. In such suffering of the innocent we are safe in saying that it is not a matter of guilt but rather the result of some transgression of the intricate, inevitable laws of nature. By these laws we live or die. As long as the body is able to function we can live in it; once it ceases to function we have to find our home in another world. At what time it ceases will vary with the individual. If we firmly believe that the life here is but a moment when compared with the eternity that awaits us, then even if life here should be of short duration that should not cause us to question God's goodness.

The question, "Why are the innocent made to suffer while so many of the guilty apparently escape?" is answered in the foregoing discussion. We cannot always ascertain who is innocent or who is guilty. Neither can we assume that suffering is always the result of personal sin. So many factors enter the picture that each case must be dealt with individually and no answer can be given that will cover every possible situation.

FOR DISCUSSION

1. Why, do you think, did God create man?
2. How does man differ from other creatures?
3. Discuss the total personality of man.
4. Discuss why the individual was so identified with the group in Old Testament times that individuality was of minor importance.
5. How did Jesus emphasize the importance of the individual?

6. How does the emphasis on the importance of the individual affect our civilization? What is its influence on the state?
7. Discuss the "why" of suffering.
8. Do you think all suffering is the result of personal sin on the part of the individual?
9. What is the interrelationship between spiritual and physical suffering? Give examples that have come to your attention.
10. How may suffering be a punishment for sin?
11. How may suffering be creative? Do you know any person who has used suffering creatively?

CHAPTER 4

What Is Sin?

Friendless and faint, with martyred steps and slow,
Faint for the flesh, but for the spirit free,
Stung by the mob that came to see the show,
The Master toiled along to Calvary;
We jibed him, as he went, with houndish glee,
Till his dimmed eyes for us did overflow;
We cursed his vengeless hands thrice wretchedly,—
And this was nineteen hundred years ago.

But after nineteen hundred years the shame
Still clings, and we have not made good the loss
That outraged faith has entered in his name.
Ah, when shall come love's courage to be strong!
Tell me, O Lord—tell me, O Lord, how long
Are we to keep Christ writhing on the cross!

EDWIN ARLINGTON ROBINSON *

A. The Meaning of Sin

Thus far in our discussion we have been using the term
"sin" assuming that we all have the same conception of what
sin is. However, we cannot assume that, because ideas on the
subject vary widely. What some accept as entirely right may
be regarded by others as wrong, and some practices accepted
as wrong by some are considered to be right by others. A male
patient referred a chaplain to Deuteronomy 22:5. The patient
was not an ordained clergyman but made very pious statements about his faith. This impressed a clergyman who visited
in the ward, and the clergyman gave that patient permission to

* From *Children of the Night,* copyright 1905. Quoted by permission
of Charles Scribner's Sons.

speak at his church when he recovered. So he chose to speak on this text regarding women's apparel. He expressed very strong feelings against women's wearing trousers and having their hair cut. When he was asked if he thought God would condemn to hell every woman who had her hair cut his prompt reply was, "Yes." He had very decided opinions concerning the sinfulness of such actions. He did not mention anything about the Seventh Commandment or that part of his illness was the result of syphilis. Since he was unmarried, he probably thought there was nothing wrong about that. (When the young clergyman became aware of the nature of this man's illness, he decided it would be better not to have him speak in his church.)

Along with such confusion there is also a lessened sense of sin. With the growth of the idea of tolerance, people have become less conscious of the conviction of sin. Many of our adults have had little or no systematic religious instruction; consequently the soul has not developed a quickened conscience. We seldom hear of any person's being put out of a Christian congregation. Individual denominational constitutions do prescribe certain ethical standards based on Scripture but, when these are violated by the individual member, the attitude of the congregation is that of Christian "charity." Perhaps that attitude has developed because there is a certain amount of competition between the churches as to size of membership, so that when a member is as a black sheep in one congregation he stands a good chance of being welcomed almost as a saint in another.

Then, also, the emphasis upon social sin may have something to do with the lessened sense of guilt on the part of the individual. He can always hide behind the group; thus, if a church shamefully underpays its pastor, secretary, or janitor, the individual member can easily shift the responsibility to the trustees or others in authority. "I'm only one member of the congregation and I can't do anything about it." The same pertains to social customs. Many an otherwise moral person will find himself involved with a group and excuse his actions by saying to himself, "When in Rome do as the Romans do." In this way he shifts the responsibility for his personal actions to the group. In childhood and adolescence we call it "the gang"; in adulthood we call it "society."

The war psychosis under which the world lived for a number of years has tended also to lower moral standards. In the movies, over the radio, and even in the "funnies" the children saw and heard killing, murder, bloodshed, and at least hints of immorality. We can hardly blame them if they got the idea that might is right, or that anything is all right as long as you can get by with it. In addition, the relaxing of parental vigilance, resulting from various causes, has shifted the responsibility for the moral training of the child from the home to the school and the church. The logical institution for moral training is the church, but again, relaxed parental vigilance is responsible for the fact that about one half of our boys and girls of grammar school age are not brought to religious instruction at a church. What moral training outside the home they are to receive will have to come largely from the public school.

During a period of war, and for a number of years afterward, there is always a lowering of moral standards. People live under abnormal tension; life is uncertain. Many die in their youth. The reaction growing out of this tension is a *laissez-faire* attitude toward morals. "We might as well enjoy ourselves as much as we can while we have a chance."

Today, religion's social emphasis has minimized the fear of hell and punishment. Hell and punishment are unpleasant words and the clergyman who repeats them too often is going to face a lot of empty pews. It is true that the old sense of sin was to a large extent very self-centered and selfish. "All

I need to be concerned about is my own salvation. If I can keep out of hell I'm all right." It is better if our consciousness of sin rises above this self-centered thinking. On the other hand the personal responsibility for sin must be emphasized because the righteousness of a social order will depend upon the righteousness of the individuals who compose that order. We cannot dismiss personal moral responsibility by shifting it to any group or organization.

THE NATURE OF SIN.—Sin is defined as "willful transgression of the divine law; neglect of the laws of morality and religion." That sin is a reality is attested by the taxes we have to pay to provide for police, detective, F.B.I., and other law-enforcing agencies, including a long list of alphabetical groups whose business it is to check up on people to keep them from cheating, lying, stealing, killing each other, and what not. Our court system is essential largely because of sin, so it also costs us what we have to pay for lawyers, judges, bailiffs, and all the other court officials. The sin bill is a high one. Wars are caused by sin also. No one will deny that wars cost money.

Since God is good and purposive, then any violation of His aims is not for the welfare of man. From a religious point of view we can say with Rall that sin is saying "No" to God. It is the block that stands in the way of what man can and ought to be. It is not only a refusal to God; it is man's refusal to himself. He denies his destiny and in so doing thwarts the purpose of his life. Instead of lifting himself [1] until he can see on a level with God, he lowers himself until he sees on the same level with those creatures that have not been created in the image of God.

Sin is transforming self-interest into selfishness. No one is blamed for enough self-interest to want to make the best of

[1] Psalms 121:1.

his abilities. But when he wants to do that regardless of the cost to others or at the price of his own integrity, his self-interest becomes selfishness. He permits deceit, hatred, greed, cruelty, and lust, to serve his selfish ends. He may accomplish what he wants, but with his selfishness he has forfeited [2] his health of soul, mind, and body. Since God is good and purposive, he sins against God also and alienates himself from Divine Fellowship.

OLD TESTAMENT VIEWS.—If men are to live together in any degree of harmony and have any fellowship with God, there must be some moral basis for that relationship. Man recognized that dire results come as a consequence of certain actions and therefore a code of conduct is necessary. A basic code of conduct in the Old Testament is the Ten Commandments,[3] given by God to Moses on Mt. Sinai. These ten may be divided into two groups. The first four, dealing with the relationship between man and God, are summed by Jesus [4] when He says, "Thou shalt love the Lord Thy God with all thy heart, and with all thy soul, and with all thy strength, and with all thy mind." The last six commandments deal with man's relationship with his fellow men and are summed by Jesus with the thought "and thy neighbor as thyself."

Any external stress naturally was interpreted by the sufferer as punishment for the remembered transgression of any or some or all of these commandments.[5] In penitence the sinner pleaded for restoration into the graces of God whose righteousness had been outraged. The joy of forgiveness was also noted by the Psalmist.[6] After restitution was made, the sinner was again in fellowship with God.

There was a divergence of opinion as to the ethical content of sin. There were those who held to the letter of the law and

[2] Matthew 16:26.
[3] Exodus 20:1-17.
[4] Luke 10:27.

[5] Psalms 10.
[6] Psalms 32.

felt that righteousness consisted of fulfilling the law in the minutest detail. Each of the Ten Commandments was divided into portions and each portion into others until the law became a very complicated affair. As an example, the Fourth Commandment became a large document in which every action on the Sabbath was prescribed. One could pour cold water into hot water, but not hot water into cold because the hot would warm the cold and that would be working. A person could walk a certain distance, "a Sabbath day's journey" without violating this commandment. Should he walk farther he would be sinning. However there were ways of getting around these prescriptions, should it be necessary, but these ways were involved and complicated.

In the Prophets we have those who found an ethical content in sin and righteousness.[7] Hosea voiced the opinion that God is more concerned about attitudes than about forms of outward conduct. But the prophets were in the minority and ceremonial perfection was emphasized [8] through the whole Old Testament.

Among specific sins often mentioned are the worship of false gods,[9] soothsaying,[10] the denial of God's power,[11] unrighteous conduct,[12] greed,[13] and voluptuousness.[14] These sins may be classified under the Ten Commandments and are especially regarded as obnoxious to God. Some of the prophets rose to such heights of ethical sensitivity that man's refusal to respond to God's love (Hosea) is regarded as sinful. Isaiah classified as sinful [15] Israel's ingratitude to God and unwillingness to do His will.

With the postexilic period, however, there came again an emphasis upon the outward in moral conduct. Sin was con-

[7] Hosea 6:6.
[8] Ezekiel 22:26.
[9] Exodus 20:22.
[10] Deuteronomy 18:10–11.
[11] Isaiah 7:5, 6, 13.
[12] II Samuel 12:9.
[13] Isaiah 5:8.
[14] Amos 6:4.
[15] Isaiah 5:1–7.

demned, not so much because it was a violation of the moral relationship between man and man, and man and God, but because of its consequences in the sinner's life. Sin would surely bring misfortune.[16]

Sin was regarded as thoughtless or malicious, and a distinction was made between the two. Thoughtless sins of youth [17] or the unconscious errors of maturity [18] were also offensive to God and must be atoned through proper sacrifice. If proper restitution were not made, these thoughtless sins would alienate the individual from God just the same as malicious transgressions.

That God punishes sin is stated generally in the Old Testament. Even though Adam is held responsible for bringing sin into the world, it is up to the individual to live his own life as relatively sinfully or righteously as he chooses. With sin comes a sense of guilt and very real disaster. Guilt and disaster cause the sinner to appeal to God for forgiveness and deliverance.

NEW TESTAMENT VIEWS.—Jesus gave a specific ethical content to the meaning of sin. He carried it from its outer appearance back into the human heart [19] and condemned the outward righteousness of the scribes and Pharisees. He regarded sin as a tendency within the individual to do things contrary to the will of God.[20] Jesus also mentioned the temptation of Satan [21] as a source of evil in the life of the individual. Thus, sin is taken from the outside to the inside and given a moral or spiritual aspect.

Christ's attitude is made available to the individual through the words of the New Testament and the experience of prayer. This spirit gives guidance within through the "I ought." When the person refuses to be guided, the con-

[16] Proverbs 1:15–19.
[17] Job 13:26.
[18] Psalms 19:12.

[19] Matthew 23:25.
[20] Matthew 7:17; 12:35.
[21] Matthew 13:19.

sequence is a feeling of guilt. That God judges and punishes sin is emphasized by Jesus throughout His teachings. Man may, to a certain extent, make restitution through repentance.[22] However, salvation can never be earned by man. Repentance is man's effort to restore himself to the graces of the good God. The actual restoration is extended to him only through the grace of God. Man may shut out the divine spirit from his life if he wishes to do so. He often does and that is sinning. John quotes Jesus [23] as saying that man may refuse or accept the divine revelation of truth and love. The divine standard of life is rejected through spiritual blindness.[24]

Thus we see what sin is and that man is constantly in need of forgiveness. The way to attain that forgiveness is offered through Christ.

B. The Consequences of Sin

Now that we have discussed what sin is, we want to consider the results of sin. Since it is saying "No" to the good and purposive will of God it must have certain results in the lives of individuals and society. Modern science has made us conscious of the fact that there is order in the universe. When the laws of nature are violated, evil results will follow. These laws are immutable. If a man gets in the way of a falling stone it will injure him. The moral laws are just as true as the laws of nature. It is no compliment to our intelligence that we have been so slow in recognizing that fact. If it were not true we could not depend upon one another at all and in place of a social structure we would have chaos.

Even our economic system is built on the assumption that there is moral order. A bank draft, after all, is nothing more than a piece of paper, practically worthless without the in-

[22] Matthew 5:23–24.   [24] John 9:41.
[23] John 5:40.

tegrity of the individual who signs his name on it. In the ministry of healing we take for granted that the pharmacist will fill the perscription exactly according to its written directions. We depend so completely upon the druggist's honesty that we take the medicine without a thought of questioning whether it has been filled according to prescription or not.

Through experience man has found that the results of sin are both personal and social. An individual cannot "hurt only himself." We are bound together by emotional, social, and economic ties to such an extent that each life, while individual, is at the same time a vital part of a larger group. When one person violates the moral laws he injures not only himself but all those who are bound to him.

PERSONAL RESULTS.—As far as the individual is concerned, sin alienates him from God.[25] No greater calamity can befall a person than to feel alone in a vast universe, because the soul of man is naturally attracted to its own spiritual element:[26] God. Since sin is rebellion against the will of God, it disturbs the natural fellowship between man and God. It does not mean that God is necessarily angry with the sinner but it does mean that the sinner has placed a barrier between himself and God. As long as the barrier remains the fellowship is disturbed. A feeling of loneliness results.

Loneliness is one of the most insidious of all spiritual stresses. Ofttimes we come upon a patient who is so ill physically that he cannot speak above a whisper. The nurse must bow down to hear his whispered need. The Psalmist found himself in the same position spiritually. Through sin he had set himself apart from God until he could not speak above a spiritual whisper. We hear him breathing forth the words: "Bow down thine ear, O Lord, and hear me."

[25] Psalms 28:1; 86:1.   [26] Psalms 42:1.

This alienation from God was also felt by the Psalmist almost physically, as though he were down in a deep pit. From the bottom of a well you can see the stars even in broad daylight. It is fortunate that God does not withdraw himself so far from the sinner that He cannot be seen. The stars can be seen through the intervening darkness and the soul that attempts to penetrate this darkness will find that fellowship can be reestablished. Thus the soul is lifted out of the pit through the grace of God into the full sunshine of His presence.

We have noticed in physical illness that the devil's brood of loneliness is selfishness, aggressiveness, inconsideration, and morbidness. The lonely patient has time for introspection. He studies his disease. It is the only thing he has to occupy his mind. After a while it becomes his chief interest. He listens for every heartbeat. His attention is centered on what he shall eat, what he shall drink, and how he shall be clothed.[27] He loses interest in the welfare of the other patients. If another receives more attention than he does, he may have an "attack" so nurses will have to give him attention. His loneliness has made him selfish.

When the individual is parted from God he becomes lonely also. He centers his attention upon his desires and sensations. His physical desires and whatever will bring pleasant physical sensations become his primary objectives. The desires of the soul are thus perverted.[28] He may feel that he is attaining satisfaction, but underneath there is always the uneasy restlessness of the soul.

The person lonely in sin must have the attention of someone. Since he has withdrawn himself from God he will have an abnormal need for others to satisfy his longings. He does not have to be organically ill to be spiritually ill. Most of the abnormal selfishness, the craving for unusual excite-

[27] Matthew 6:24.   [28] Romans 1:23-32.

ment and sensations, may be attributed to the selfishness which grows out of the loneliness of the soul that is alienated from its God. That soul does not know the meaning of His gift of peace.[29]

The soul alienated from God also becomes aggressive, either toward God or toward other persons. It is dissatisfied alone and must have companionship. It tries to find that companionship in normal healthy friendship, but still this is not sufficient. It has to have more attention. Individuals who crave pampering are just lonely souls trying to find satisfaction.

The lonely person may become very inconsiderate of relatives, friends, nurses, doctors, and others. The family usually bears the brunt of this sin. If this person is a patient in a hospital, charges of a lack of love will be made against the relatives who do not show enough interest to satisfy the craving. One mother actually insisted that her daughter quit her job in order to be with the mother constantly while she was recovering from an operation. When it was explained to her that it was against the rules of the hospital to have someone constantly present she became quite angry. Older persons sometimes make abnormal demands upon their children and inconsiderateness is one of the besetting devils bred in the loneliness of old age.

Loneliness does make a person very inconsiderate of others. The lonely patient doesn't bother to remember that the nurse has other patients to care for. He complains about a lack of attention. "I can ring and it takes an hour before anyone shows up, and that doctor of mine must have altogether forgotten that I exist." When he is asked confidentially about the welfare of other patients in the room he will tell you that they are getting along perfectly all right; that there is nothing wrong with them.

[29] John 14:27.

The person who is spiritually lonely becomes inconsiderate of God also. He has withdrawn from God and is prone to blame God for his predicament. In a moment when the conscience is quickened and would urge him back to fellowship, he may deny the promptings of his soul with the thought, "God does not care for me. If He did, He would not permit these things to happen to me." He tries to rationalize his attitude by blaming it on God.

Or he may blame it on a minister. One such lonely person made the remark, "All preachers are crooks." Upon further inquiry it was found that as a youngster he was forced to go to church. It just happened in that instance that the clergyman appeared to be dishonest. This gave him an excuse to stop going to church. As time went on he alienated himself from God, became very irreligious, and denied the existence of God. In an attempt to rationalize his situation, he blamed it on all preachers. It is sometimes said that all atheists recognize the presence of God before they die. That was not the case with this man. To the end, despite the urging of his family, he maintained that there is no God and apparently refused to pray or in any way consider His presence. He hardened his heart through loneliness to such an extent that he was entirely inconsiderate of the feelings either of God or of his relatives.

When the inconsiderate sinner decides to pray he thinks God must come post haste to answer his call. Jesus pictured such persons in the parables of the man who knocked at midnight [30] and of the unjust judge.[31] In the first parable, the man who knocked at midnight expected his neighbor to arise immediately and give him bread. But why should he? This man had never come to see him in the daytime, there was no bond of fellowship between them. The neighbor was not obligated. The one who is a stranger in the spiritual palace of

[30] Luke 11:5-13.　　　　　　　[31] Luke 18:2-8.

the King can hardly expect the King to recognize him immediately and grant him favors. In the second parable the Lord teaches such a person who prays to keep at it until he is heard, even as the widow persisted in her prayers to the judge. The inconsiderate sinner is apt in a moment of spiritual dawn to expect God to come immediately, even though he has never apologized (repented) for the treatment he has offered Him.

The lonely patient may also become morbid, brooding over his condition and yet unwilling to do anything about it. His sickly estate becomes chronic. At times he may wish that he were in health again; then he thinks of the responsibilities that come with health and because of his lethargy he prefers ill health to responsibilities. He may express a desire to get up and say that he wishes he were well again but, when the physician or nurse suggests that he make the attempt, he will have an "attack" or say that he is afraid the exertion will be fatal. Of course, such a patient is psychopathic, but a psychopathic patient is none the less ill and his loneliness has been one of the main factors contributing to his condition.

The spiritually ill person may also become spiritually lazy. He realizes that he is ill and often expresses regret over his state. But still he does nothing about it. When the suggestion is made by well-meaning persons that he go to church, he may say that he will, but he doesn't. The restlessness of his soul causes him to rebel against this apartness from God; occasionally he may express the wish that he were better or that he lived a different life, but when someone suggests practical ways through which he may relieve his stress he will have excuses. Actually, he does not care to assume the responsibilities attached to the life of a person who is in fellowship with God.

These, then, are some of the devils bred by spiritual loneliness. Sin alienates the soul from God, and the sinner who refuses to do anything about it becomes spiritually psychopathic. The "censor," or the conscience, becomes ever less vociferous in its rebellion against this state of apartness unless it is quickened by some spiritual experience. The soul is damned by sin. The creature of the Creator lives its life apart from Him.

SOCIAL RESULTS.—Just as sin ravishes the soul, mind, and body, so it has its evil effect upon society. As it separates man from God it also separates man from man. Human association should be a rich experience, but sin enters the picture and makes it sordid. Child labor, war, venereal disease, political corruption, poverty are some of the effects of sin upon society. The sin of greed motivates the industrialist who would employ, because they will work cheaply, the children who should be going to school or enjoying the sunshine. War may be the result of the sins of pride, greed, and selfishness on the part of those who guide the destinies of men. Venereal diseases are the outgrowth of the abuse of a human function that should be noble and pure. Political corruption is caused by the sins of carelessness and indifference on the part of the people and selfishness and lust for power on the part of conscienceless individuals who promote their own interests above those of society.

Poverty is one of the great cancers of our civilization.[32] Even in prosperous days when the income of the nation reaches unprecedented heights, there are still millions living below the poverty line in hovels unfit for animals. Yet some landlords charge high rents for the hovels; unscrupulous politicians may prevent building projects because the politicians are either supported by the landlords or own the unfit dwellings themselves. Cold-blooded men exact their pound of flesh because the law allows it and are hailed in certain circles as upright citizens because they amass wealth. The besetting sin

[32] Amos 2:6.

of greed [33] is also one of the causes of the disputes between labor and industry, when the one side tries to hold down or lower wages, and when the other tries to gain increases for some trades and skills while others are overlooked. Fairminded business and labor leaders will try to adjust their demands in such a way that the greater benefit will accrue to the larger number of individuals.

God has provided us with a beautiful, bountiful earth that can be made to supply the needs of all the people who live here. But greed, selfishness, and covetousness have caused men to take advantage of their fellow men and this is another cause of poverty that cannot be overlooked.

Society can and does sin just as the individual. In such cases it is comparatively easy for the individual to assuage his conscience for the suffering that such sin has caused by hiding behind the shield of group responsibility. But he is nonetheless responsible. The individuals of a society that permits unnecessary suffering are just as guilty as an individual who inflicts suffering on another.

A harvest of hatred and suspicion results when nations, indifferent to their international obligations, employ deceit, and are callous toward the just rights of others. They turn the earth that God intended to be good and friendly to the existence of man into a place of oppression and sorrow. Nations, too, must suffer for the sins they commit.[34]

The word "sin" in the original Greek means to shoot an arrow and miss the mark. Sin is missing the mark, working contrary to the good and purposive will of God. Whether in the life of an individual or a group or a nation, the results of sin always spell failure.

---

[33] Amos 4:1.   [34] Galatians 6:7.

For Discussion

1. How are moral standards established?
2. Are traditions and customs related in any way to conscience?
3. Is it wise to say to anyone, "Let your conscience be your guide"?
4. Discuss the nature of sin.
5. How did the concept "sin" develop an ethical content?
6. Do you think what a person does is more important than what he thinks? Explain.
7. What are sins of omission? Sins of commission?
8. How can a person cope with a feeling of guilt?
9. What are some personal consequences of sin? What are some social consequences of sin?
10. Why do we say that loneliness is one of the most insidious of the spiritual stresses?
11. What are some of the results of loneliness?
12. Why do we say that sin is one of our most costly luxuries?

CHAPTER 5

What Is Salvation?

A MAN APPEARED

How curious that men have always feared
The work of their own hands! The Chaldees bent
Before their craven gods, to whom they lent
Imagined powers, till a man appeared.
When Abraham arose the heavens cleared,
And God, his friend, went with him where he went,
As in a wilderness he pitched his tent
And through untraveled ways his footsteps steered.

But still men fear! Armies they fear, and fleets,
And winged battalions, till they pause and gasp
Before a bomb their tiny hands have made.
God, send the leader who serenely meets
The future with his hand within Thy clasp
And toward new worlds advances unafraid!

HELEN A. RANLETT *

From what we have already studied concerning the nature
of man and the nature and results of sin we readily see that
man's estate is not very promising without the assistance of a
God who loves us. Rall tells us that religion has three aspects :
it is a faith that we hold, a life that we live, and a help that we
receive. Salvation is God extending a helping hand to man.
It is the spiritual arm of the Almighty lifting the individual
out of the pit into the clear air of a sunny day.

A. The Meaning of Salvation

There were times when the individual's salvation was considered as being other-worldly. A person did not have to be

* Reprinted by permission of *The Christian Century.*

so much concerned about conditions in this world. Christians could be browbeaten in poverty and even lack the necessities of life; that was all right because some day they would get to Heaven, and then *everything* would be all right. Or an individual could go ahead and live his life in sin, just so he was converted a few minutes before he died. The example of the repentant malefactor [1] was emphasized. That he got into Heaven by the skin of his teeth was sufficient. All that he missed in life because he lived it apart from God was not mentioned. The eagerness to provide a heaven where all would be well took the attention from a full, abundant life here and now.[2]

Humanism arising in the Renaissance took the opposite point of view. It laid the emphasis altogether on the here and now. The machine age made all kinds of luxuries available for man. Humanism took the viewpoint that the important thing in life was to get as many of these luxuries as possible, and to live handsomely here in this world.

Both of these views have truth in them. Jesus emphasized the importance of the eternal life.[3] The hope for a reward in eternity is a motivating factor in Christian ethics. That sin will be punished in eternity is also stated by Jesus.[4] The early disciples and apostles also preached divine judgment.[5]

There is also truth in the humanistic point of view. When the missionaries approach people in foreign lands they realize that they can hardly convert those who have empty stomachs. The full preaching of the Gospel has been supplemented by an educational program, medical ministrations, and political and industrial guidance that will raise the standard of living. No one will deny that man has the right to a decent life in this world.

[1] Luke 23:39–43.
[2] John 10:10.
[3] Matthew 5:12.

[4] Luke 6:23–25.
[5] Romans 2:3.

FROM WHAT IS MAN SAVED?—We see the word "save" in "salvation." Now we would consider from what man is to be saved. Human needs call for salvation. God's love is the answer to that call.

Man must be saved from himself. The story of human relationships down the centuries is a very bloody one. The pages of history are crimson, with the exception of those written through the influence of Jesus and those who have shared his spirit. Sin has made great inroads into human relationships and man has been very cruel to his fellow men.

With scientific development, ever more power has been given to man. He may use these newly found powers either for the benefit of mankind or for its destruction. Thus man hangs between heaven and hell, and it is the business of religion to save him from the hell he may bring upon himself. This is not an easy task because sin has a strong hold on human personalities. Some men gain authority who have very little religion. Feeling no responsibility toward God, they may devise evil to satisfy their own vanity, and so all society suffers. As long as free people grant authority to irreligious individuals they can expect such results.

In the economic sphere of civilization also, man needs to be saved from himself. It seems that every invention that could provide man with more leisure for the nobler pursuits of life is used to make more demands upon his time and physical resources. The trend toward materialism causes him to center his attention upon things, and economic greed makes these things hard to get. The greater the demand for a certain thing, the higher the price. Man makes plums and holds them just beyond his own reach. He stretches his arm as far as he can, and if he cannot reach them he is tempted to get the plums by other than ethical means.

Man alone will never attain the ethical or moral heights that are within the realm of his achievement. It is here that the spirit of Christ reaches into his life and makes him capable of what he by nature could not attain. Left to himself, man destroys himself with the very instruments that might bring him a better life. When the aeroplane was developed its potentialities for easy, convenient travel were readily recognized. By means of it man could circle the globe in a very short time. Making travel easy and convenient, it could be the means of making nations and races better acquainted with each other. But it could also be used to destroy, and to that use it was developed and devoted until it has become one of man's most terrible instruments of destruction. Millions have been made homeless and countless lives have been lost through bombs dropped by men from aeroplanes. Any scientific knowledge may thus be perversely used. As man continues to find and develop the latent powers of the universe he may become ever more dangerous to himself. Man needs to be saved from himself.

Man needs to be saved from the personal results of sin; from poverty, sickness, and death. Poverty, to a large extent, may be the result of sin; certainly not poverty arising from disaster or disability. Poverty in its turn breeds sin so those children raised in poverty are underprivileged. It is true that much poverty can be attributed to the sins of laziness and carelessness. The use of intoxicating liquors and the practice of gambling account also for poverty. So we can say that the individual often brings poverty upon himself and his family. Physical handicaps also contribute to the poverty of some in an economic system that is highly competitive. Yet it can be said that these are causes of poverty from which man can be saved. This salvation may mean work, effort, and sacrifice on the part of those who would apply the principles of Jesus to daily living. But the possibility remains and it can be done. Man's conscience must be quickened until it rebels against the sins that rob so many of their birthright.

Man needs to be saved from sickness. Sickness is commonly thought of only in the physical realm, but sickness is really threefold, spiritual, mental, and physical. Spiritual anguish is often more unbearable than physical pain and may be a contributing factor in physical illness. But a person does not necessarily have to be physically ill to suffer spiritually. Much hopelessness, frustration, and craving for excitement are results of an impoverished, sickly soul. Physicians tell us that a constantly increasing percentage of their patients have nothing wrong with them organically; they are suffering from either mental or spiritual illness. Man can be saved from spiritual suffering. When the soul is in fellowship with God it is at peace.[6]

Mental suffering is usually designated by the terms worry, anxiety, sorrow, and a feeling of insecurity or of frustration. Mental suffering causes much anguish from which man needs to be saved, and the Christian religion offers a way of salvation. False pride, common ignorance, and vanity are often in the background of mental suffering. The individual can, to a great degree, help himself overcome these sins. The spirit of Christ enables him to have faith and trust in the all-wise providence of God.[7]

In the physical realm also there is a vast amount of unnecessary suffering. Medical science has conquered many diseases and added years to the average life span. There is yet a great field to be mastered and medical scientists are making ever greater advances. We see some of the results of these achievements here in America, but there are many countries where such advances are virtually unknown. Medical missions undertake the tremendous task of relieving unnecessary suffering in these lands, but their efforts are inadequate because there are neither enough missionaries nor enough resources available to meet the need. People are not concerned deeply

[6] John 14:26-31.   [7] Romans 8:28; Matthew 6:33.

enough to support medical missions sufficiently to meet these needs.

Methods of sanitation and of other types of disease prevention, if made generally effective, could prevent much of this unnecessary suffering. But again, this becomes a matter of economics, and greed stands in the way. Those who have the means to promote such humanitarian projects lose interest when they realize there is little or no material profit in it for them. Philanthropists do devote large sums to such purposes, but again we must say that the effort is inadequate.

Even in America where we enjoy the highest standard of living in the world, adequate medical care is beyond the financial reach of many. This may be because there is so much else that people need and cannot put off getting, while they can put off getting medical care. They suffer and die needlessly because they do not have the knowledge of or the wherewithal to provide essential medical care, or are careless and do not provide themselves with health insurance. Cities and communities tolerate districts that breed disease and housing conditions that undermine good health. Men and women must often work in unhealthful surroundings; those who are responsible and could improve conditions do not, because such improvements cost money. Certain laws exist that prescribe minimum health conditions in places where people are employed, and as standards of living improve these conditions improve also. Safety measures in industry reduce the accident and death rate in dangerous occupations. Many industrial plants employ nurses and doctors to care for the health of the personnel; advances in this direction will further reduce the toll of unnecessary accidents and will be conducive to better health. In this connection we should also mention that social agencies, private and public, are gaining ever more recognition, and altruists are entering these fields of service in increasing numbers. The standard of living and the education of the masses must somehow be raised so that they will take advantage of the results of medical research and the means of preventing disease.

Man also needs to be saved from physical suffering that is caused by personal sins, the transgression of the moral and spiritual laws. These set him against God, and his flesh rebels through suffering that could be avoided. Someone has said, unjustly, that since ministers have gotten away from preaching sin, the psychiatrists and medical doctors are taking over the field. The clergy are very much aware of the vast amount of suffering that is caused by sin and therefore do not minimize its results.

WHY SHOULD MAN BE SAVED?—Someone has asked, "Of what use is good health if it is not put to good use?" There is no special merit in just existing in this world over a long period of years and enjoying good health. Methuselah is said to have lived to the age of 969 years, and yet the Scripture gives you the import of his life in four short verses.[8] What a person like David or Paul or Pasteur or Lincoln could have done with so many years! If man is saved he ought to be saved for some purposeful action.

Man's environment consists chiefly of three things: God, his fellow men, and the physical universe. In the parable about good manners in the Kingdom of God,[9] the rude guest did not take the wishes of his host into consideration. He would dine at the host's table and yet be unconcerned about what the host thinks or whether his fellow diners have a place and are served. We are all feasting at the banquet table of life and God is the great and good Host. If we accept His hospitality we should also be concerned about His pleasure.

God is a part of man's environment.[10] Man must adjust himself to God. If he is saved he ought to be saved to do God's

---

[8] Genesis 5:21, 25-27.
[9] Luke 14:7-11.
[10] Acts 17:28.

will. There is no special merit in inactive salvation.[11] So we can see first of all that man is saved in order that he may help establish the Kingdom of God on earth. Saved men and women must have a vital part in that program. If the will of God, as it is revealed in His Word, is to be done upon the earth, saved men and women are those who will do it.

The second important factor in his environment is his fellow men. When a person is saved he will certainly want to share his satisfaction with others and he will be concerned about their welfare. No man can live to himself alone. We are bound to each other with social, economic, and spiritual ties to such an extent that each life is influenced by others.[12] The Christian cannot be unconcerned about the welfare of his fellow men. There are no racial or national limits to that concern. He feels that there is a place upon the earth for all the people whom God has created and they are all potentially His children. In his dealings with his fellow men he will treat them according to their potentialities. He knows that the important thing is not what man came from but rather what man is and can be. When God becomes his Father, his fellow men become his brethren. He will do what he can for the welfare of the other members of God's family.

The third important factor in man's environment is the universe in which he lives. Since he is better endowed than any other creature, he is better able to adapt himself to the everchanging conditions of the world. It is the purpose of religion to help him feel at home here by explaining the world in spiritual terms. Once man understands that the universe is friendly to his existence, he finds that there are many things for him to do here. There is beauty in the earth, and purpose in nature. There is order in the universe, and freshness, purity, and life all around him. All these have been marred and scarred by sin. He is saved not only to enjoy what there

[11] James 2:17.   [12] Matthew 5:13-16.

is here to enjoy, but to bring forth and out of the earth all the potentialities there are. As these potentialities are limited, it is vital that they be used in such ways as to assure the widest benefits for all the people. The world must be mastered by man,[13] not man by the world, if he is to live life to the fullest.

Salvation then for the individual should mean in a measure a realization of his spiritual potentialities. He should be a person who is easy to get along with and who lives his life as a child of God ought to live it. Someone has said that a Christian can be compared to a Rome Beauty apple. The Rome Beauty is a converted crab apple.

B. The Means of Salvation

Man has tried in various ways to save himself from the results of sin. Among people everywhere there is some effort to rise above or beyond the present state. The soul of man reaches out toward the element from which it emanated. We will not go into the efforts toward salvation being made by people other than Christians. This field is very wide and is a study in itself.

In the Old Testament man tried to save himself by righteous acts, rituals, and ceremonies. Much tradition and superstition grew around these rituals, with emphasis being laid upon the acts rather than the ethical content. The sinner believed that as long as he followed certain rules and regulations imposed by the clergy, who were supposed to know what pleases God, he would be saved. Then there were also those who felt that by denying themselves everything physical they would be well pleasing to God and thus merit salvation. John the Baptist, the last prophet of the Old Testament and the first of the New,[14] belongs in this category. By withdrawing from the world and treating his body and all that pertains to

[13] Genesis 1:26.   [14] Matthew 3:4.

it with utter contempt, he felt that he was being righteous in the eyes of God. There are many who still feel the same way about it.

When Jesus refused to emphasize asceticism He was severely criticized.

This denial of the flesh was carried over into the Christian way of life also and found its expression in monasticism. But man found that by works alone he could not save himself, try as he would. He found that sin was more than he could handle by himself. Man tried also to save himself through intellectual achievement. Salvation became a matter of knowledge of this world and of God. Theology became a science. Man tried to rationalize God. Health cults grew out of this viewpoint, but that still left the soul of man uneasy and without the peace he sought.

From the beginning of time God through His great love was determined that man should be saved from sin and its results. He must be saved personally and socially. God revealed himself progressively to mankind, and as man grew in spiritual perception He revealed ever more of His will. That revelation reached its crucial point in Jesus Christ.

Through Jesus we know that man must be saved personally, as we shall see in the next chapter.[15] He must be made over until the will of God becomes his chief concern and his way of life.[16] Where he might have been weak and vacillating he becomes strong and sure of himself. He has found ideals that are worth striving for and are worth dying for. He is certain that he has found the truth and that truth relieved his soul of anxiety.[17] He is restored to the fellowship with God which is his rightful heritage. He is no longer a slave of the world or his own desires; he is the master that God intended him to be. He knows the importance of the influence of hered-

[15] John 3:3.
[16] Matthew 6:33.

[17] John 8:32.

ity and environment on his character and so is able to make the best of whatever his portion in this world is.

To summarize, then, we may say that salvation is not achieved solely through man's own efforts.[18] Through God's grace the spirit of Christ permeates his being and that spirit makes it possible for him to be saved. In other words, man makes the effort and God reaches toward man with his love.

This salvation also has social implications, as we have seen. Man is saved not only for himself but also for the welfare of his fellow men. Christ has promised His spirit to those who believe.[19] Man's faith in God is the medium through which he appropriates the merits of Jesus Christ and the spirit of Christ. That spirit urges him to emulate, as far as his abilities will permit, the life of his Saviour. In this manner he establishes his fellowship with his fellow men. He is not only interested in doing God's will toward others, but also in seeing that it is done by others. Thus right relationships are established between man and man.

For Discussion

1. Discuss the meaning of the word "Salvation." Look it up in a dictionary.
2. Do you think it is possible for a person to save himself for an abundant life here and hereafter?
3. What is other-worldliness in religious thought? What does humanism emphasize?
4. Why does man need to be saved? Is he not getting along all right as it is?
5. What disorganizing factors are brought to bear on human life that we could get along very well without?
6. How may man be saved from mental suffering?
7. What are three important influences in man's environment to which he must adjust himself if he would live the abundant life?

[18] Matthew 26:41.   [19] John 14:16-21.

8. What part do good works play in the process of salvation?
   What part do faith and repentance play in the processes of
   salvation? What is repentance?
9. How does the grace of God, manifested in Jesus, help save
   man?

CHAPTER 6

What Do Christians Think of Christ?

THE SONG OF A HEATHEN

If Jesus Christ is a man,—
    And only a man—I say
That of all mankind I cleave to him
    And to him I will cleave alway.

If Jesus Christ is a god—
    And the only God—I swear
I will follow Him through heaven and hell,
    The earth, the sea, and the air.
                    RICHARD WATSON GILDER *

Many Christians think of Christ and God interchangeably, first of one, then of the other, without much distinction. We have already discussed the revelation of God through Christ. Christ is called the Son of God. He is thought of as both human and divine, though in different ways. One early churchman identified the human and divine so closely as to speak of Mary as the Mother of God. More moderately another great Christian said that in Christ was all of God that could be put into a human life. A small group of Christians denies His deity, although these Christians are not looked upon with favor by the great majority.

Christ is thought of as an example. He had lived life fully and well, and we might well live like Him. He is the pioneer of life.[1] Christians likewise call Him Lord and Master.[2] It is interesting to note that Lord is the name used for God in much of the Old Testament.

---

* Quoted by permission of and arrangement with Houghton Mifflin Co., authorized publishers.
[1] Acts 3:15.   [2] John 13:13; Acts 2:36.

A. His Saviourhood

Perhaps more than anything else, Jesus is thought of as Saviour.[3] The Hebrews had sometimes spoken of God as their Saviour.[4] The common people all over the world in recent years have looked on their national leaders as saviors. There seems to be a confused awareness that something is terribly wrong, and a dependence on someone to make it right. The Hebrews looked to God to save them.

THE SALVATION OF ISRAEL.—Many of the Jews of Jesus' day looked to the Christ as the Saviour.[5] They thought of salvation in national terms and believed the Christ would restore their national independence. That hope is understandable as we look at the nations of Europe which were also overrun by a great military power. But in the case of Israel there was an added incentive. They were convinced, in a peculiar sense, that they were God's chosen people and that He would work through them to bring about His rule over all the nations of the earth. He would send, they believed, His Christ to establish His Kingdom; that is, restore the kingdom of Israel.

There also were those religious leaders who thought of the Christ as a supernatural person. Jesus' disciples hoped that He was the promised one.[6]

There were various views as to how this restoration was to be accomplished. Some thought that the restoration would be by military means. Others believed there would be divine intervention and that the good people had only faithfully to observe the law. Others felt that the coming of the Kingdom would be hastened by living a good life. In fact, there was a

[3] Matthew 1:21.
[4] Psalms 106:21; Isaiah 43:3.
[5] This name was applied originally to the Israelite kings. Christ comes from the Greek word meaning anointed. The term later became a proper name applied only to the hoped-for redeemer.
[6] Luke 24:21; Acts 1:6.

saying that if everyone for a single day would live a life of perfect obedience to God the Kingdom would come.

THE SALVATION OF SINNERS.—Thus we see that salvation was early thought of in connection with the forgiveness of sins. When people began to think of the salvation of the individual person instead of the restoration of the nation, the idea of salvation from sin went with it. The work of Jesus is associated with the remission of sins.[7]

SALVATION IN CHRIST'S SUFFERING.—Jesus' work of salvation has always been connected with His suffering and death. One immediately thinks of the beautiful verses from Isaiah [8] which are read in many churches during the Christmas season. The Isaian verses give us a picture of a servant of God: a servant who suffers in attempting to carry out the will of God; a servant who, through his suffering, bears the consequences of the sins of many people. There is reason to believe that those early followers of Jesus, and Jesus himself, had this ideal of the suffering servant in mind.[9]

Perhaps you have wondered how the suffering and death of Christ worked for your salvation. Many have, and some have worked out explanations.

A SACRIFICE FOR SIN.—Among the earliest ideas was that the death of Christ was a sacrifice. Those who were familiar with the temple ritual thought of the shedding of blood as necessary for the remission of sin. Just how or why this was necessary would not need to be explained. For generations people had come to Jerusalem with sacrificial animals as expiation for sin. Jesus now became the final sacrifice. This is the point of view in the Epistle to the Hebrews.

AS A RANSOM.—Another theory is that the death of Christ was a ransom. Jesus himself spoke of His death as a ran-

[7] Acts 3:26; 10:43.　　　　[9] Luke 24:26, 45-46.
[8] Isaiah 52:13-53:12.

som.[10] Mankind was in the power of Satan. The death of Christ was in the nature of a payment for their release. Of course Satan gained nothing by accepting such a ransom, for at the death of Jesus He was Himself released from the power and possession of Satan.

AN EXPRESSION OF GOD'S JUSTICE.—Another explanation of the death of Christ is from the point of view of retributive justice. Since God is just, He could not forgive sin without showing His wrath toward it. God's wrath, which was demanded by justice, would if directed against mankind destroy all humanity. God did not want to destroy humanity, but since He was infinite He could bear the sins of humanity Himself. No further punishment, therefore, for sin is necessary.

All these explanations of the death of Christ rest on the initial assumption that sin is something that can be transferred from one person to another. In other words, sin is an impersonal thing. We sometimes jokingly say that we wish someone would take our cold so we would no longer be troubled with it. It is such a transfer in the spiritual realm that these theories indicate. But some persons believe that sin cannot be transferred from one personality to another any more than cancer, for example, can be transferred from one person to another. They therefore seek an explanation of the death of Christ as a means of salvation in harmony with a view which does not separate sin from personality.

VICTIM OF MAN'S SIN.—The death of Christ may be thought of as a result of man's wrongdoing. Certain religious leaders of His day were jealous of His religious leadership among the masses. Certain wealthy men feared Him because He had driven their stock from the temple where they were selling it at a huge profit. The governor tried to hold his posi-

[10] Mark 10:45.

tion by giving in to the demands of the people. One of Jesus' disciples, weary of fighting for an ideal, had told the police where He was so that they might arrest Him. Jesus had died because of these sins.

AN EXPRESSION OF GOD'S LOVE.—Saint Paul has told us that God was in Christ, reconciling the world unto Himself.[11] Some Christians have thought that these words suggest why it was necessary for Christ to die. Whereas the justice theory indicates that the attitude of God toward man was changed by the death of Christ, Paul's expression indicates that it is the attitude of man toward God that has changed. There is something to be said for this view. The attitude of God did not need to be changed, but the attitude of man toward God did need to be changed. God's love for the world is a constant love.[12] The death of Jesus on the Cross becomes an expression of God's love. It is a love that stops at nothing in order that man might be saved. It took the death of Christ to convince man of God's love for him.

Whichever view a person takes of the atonement, he is convinced that Christ did something for him and that His death was somehow necessary in order to do that. Gratitude for this deed of Christ has led countless thousands to devote all that they are and have to Him.

B. The Significance of Christ

When Jesus called His first disciple, a new thing came to pass upon the earth: a fellowship came into being. The idea of fellowship was very strong with the first Christians.[13] Some think this very close relationship was a continuation of the way Jesus had lived with His disciples.

[11] II Corinthians 5:19.
[12] John 3:16.
[13] Acts 2:42; 4:32.

Fellowship with Jesus continued after His death and resurrection.[14] Jesus was the first representative of a new type of humanity—the ideal man through whom a spiritual humanity was created.[15] Some believe that man was perfect in the beginning and fell through disobedience and sin. Saint Paul seemed to feel that man was created an earthly being[16] and that the second man, referring to Christ, is of heaven. The first man became a living soul, the second a life-giving spirit.

The fellowship of which this life-giving spirit is the center has continued to grow. It outgrew the little group of disciples. It grew beyond the bound of the national life—"unto Samaria and unto the uttermost parts of the earth."[17] It now includes hundreds of millions. The members of this fellowship are in all parts of the earth.

THE HEAD OF THE CHURCH.—In this fellowship Christ is the recognized Head.[18] A new thought movement in Colossae in the days of Saint Paul failed to interest the Christians because it did not give Christ first place.[19] The early Christians were not averse to accepting Greek ideas that called Christ the Word.[20] This was because the Greeks had no concepts similar to Christ. The Word was the highest being they knew.[21] The Word in Greek thinking referred to the creator, who was sometimes thought of as not being the same as God. The early Christians used the new ideas which gave Christ first place and rejected any which seemed to deny Him primacy.

The headship seemed more than that of a principal individual. Saint Paul often indicated an organic union as though Christ were the directing intelligence and motivating spirit,

[14] Matthew 28:20; 18:20; Acts 2:33.
[15] I Corinthians 15:45–49.
[16] Compare Genesis 2:7, 8 and Genesis 1:26, 27.
[17] Acts 1:8.
[18] Colossians 1:18.
[19] Colossians 2:19.
[20] John 1:14.
[21] Read John 1:1–14 with this in mind.

and the Church the body which did the physical work in the material universe. Today that earthly body is divided. Maybe that is the reason why Christ does not do more work in the world today. It is important to keep in mind that there is one Head.

Jesus accepted the thought that He occupied the central position in the Kingdom of God. That thought was confirmed at the baptism.[22] He acknowledged Peter's confession that He was the Christ.[23] He believed that He was the means of God's revelation.[24] In the view of Saint Paul, Jesus does the final work of redemption.[25] In the view of Saint John, He has a unique fellowship with God and brings a unique relationship to man.[26] Jesus is central in Christian living and thinking. The young Christians in conference at Oslo in the summer of 1947 were right when they displayed in Filadelfia Hall the words JESUS CHRIST IS LORD. The oft repeated words are true. Jesus Christ will be Lord of all, or He will not be Lord at all.

THE ELDER BROTHER.—The creeds of the church recognize the humanity of Jesus. One of the oldest creeds, the Athanasian, which is said to embody the form of the Trinity which Augustine taught, says, "For the right Faith is, that we believe and confess that our Lord Jesus Christ, the son of God, is God and Man; God of the Substance of the Father begotten before the worlds: and man of the substance of His mother born in the world; perfect God and perfect Man: of a reasonable soul and human flesh subsisting." The most recent statement is in the Westminster Confession. It says that "two whole, perfect, and distinct natures, the Godhead and Manhood, were unseparably joined together in one person, without conversion, composition, or confusion."

[22] Luke 3:22.
[23] Matthew 16:16, 17.
[24] Luke 10:22.
[25] Galatians 4:4, 5.
[26] John 3:13–15.

The ponderous words of the creeds may prevent us from getting the real significance of the thought. More intimate are the words of a pastor, "He is a human brother to the rest of us." [27] This is the way many persons felt about Him in His earthly ministry. We refresh our minds with the picture presented by Mark. Jesus was a carpenter at Nazareth, known as Jesus the son of Joseph. At thirty He began an itinerant ministry. He sat down by a Samaritan well, thirsty and weary. Dust settled on His sandaled feet as He walked the weary miles of His Judean journeys. He pursued the same hopes and suffered the same disappointments as other men. Perhaps we have suffered no hardship which He did not encounter and have been baffled by no temptation which He did not meet. Of course the marvelous thing about it was that though this was true, yet He was without sin.[28] Other men since the beginning of history have felt remorse for good deeds omitted, and sorrow for misdeeds committed. In the consciousness of Jesus there is no remorse. Dr. Edgar Helms, who was pastor of the Church of All Nations in Boston, used to say that Jesus was God's idea of what a man ought to be.

It may seem strange to us that a person can be thought of as both God and man. However, most Christians have so thought of Jesus through the centuries. The only difficulty has been to explain how the two natures, human and divine, are united in one. That difficulty has caused a great deal of disunion and dissension, but is not now a live issue. We have already discussed in Chapter 2 the Divine phase of Christ's nature.

For most Christians, the greatest significance lies in the saviourhood of Christ. Many refer to Him simply as "our Saviour." Many feel close to Him because they can look to Him as one of ourselves, one who has gone on ahead to inter-

[27] Compare Paul's words in Romans 8:29.
[28] Hebrews 4:15.

cede for us. Many others are thrilled by the greatness of His ethical teachings. For many He stands in the place of God. Either they understand God better because He is like Christ, or they think of Christ as God.

The first few verses of the letter to the Hebrews express some of the thoughts which Christians have concerning Jesus as the revelation of God. After we read them we ponder on their meaning. We wonder, for example, what can be the meaning of "the very image of His substance." A group of young people were holding an Easter sunrise service on a broad rock at the top of a cliff. There had been considerable rain, the river had overflowed, and water was standing in the adjacent field. A few minutes after sunrise, the clouds parted and the sun shone in all its springtime splendor. The broad surface of water in the field reflected the sun and the parted clouds. If one had not seen the surrounding fields, it would have been difficult to tell which was sun and which was reflection. This experience has helped this writer to understand how Christ could be the very image of God's substance, how it is that when he sees Christ he can see God.

For Discussion

1. Are people more likely to look for a national savior than an individual savior? Why?
2. Can a nation be saved unless its individual citizens are saved? Explain. Do you think the Jewish nation discovered this by experience?
3. Below are listed some things from which people have wanted to be saved. Which salvation is most fundamental? In other words, would salvation from one of them open the way to salvation from all the others? Which one? Ignorance, slavery, poverty, sin, disease.
4. How do the suffering and death of Jesus work for salvation from sin? Discuss the view which appeals most to you.

5. Are there indications that the disciples continued to live on the same financial arrangement that they had when Jesus was with them? See Acts 2:44–47; 4:32–37; Luke 8:1–3. Do you think this financial arrangement depended on the spiritual fellowship?

6. In what ways can Christ be thought of as the Head of the Church?

7. If Christians made Jesus central in their living and thinking, what changes would take place in the city where you live? In your life?

8. Does it help you to feel that Jesus lived the life of a human being? In what ways does it help you?

9. Have you ever tried to understand how Jesus Christ could be God? If this chapter has helped you, explain how.

CHAPTER 7

What Is the Value of Prayer?

Lord, what a change within us one short hour
  Spent in thy presence will avail to make!
  What heavy burdens from our bosoms take!
What parched grounds refresh as with a shower!

We kneel, and all around us seems to lower;
  We rise, and all, the distant and the near,
  Stands forth in sunny outline, brave and clear,
We kneel, how weak! we rise, how full of power!
          RICHARD CHENEVIX TRENCH

As I enter here from day to day,
And leave my burden at this minster gate,
Kneeling in prayer, and not ashamed to pray,
The tumult of the time disconsolate
To inarticulate murmurs dies away,
While the eternal ages watch and wait.
          HENRY WADSWORTH LONGFELLOW *

A. What Is Prayer?

Prayer is the conversation of man with God.[1] For the Christian, it is a conversation with God for the purpose of praising Him, thanking Him, and asking Him for those things that are necessary for the soul, mind, and body. Prayer is the means by which the Christian keeps in fellowship with his God. One could not live in the same house with another person for any length of time without talking over mutual problems or expressing affection. If man is in fellowship

* Quoted by permission of and arrangement with Houghton Mifflin Co., authorized publishers.
[1] Matthew 6:5-8.

with God, the same thing is true. Prayer is a necessity. Man's desire for fellowship makes it absolutely necessary for him to pray. God also uses this medium to reach down into human life. So prayer is not only an effort on man's part, but through it the grace of God is also extended.

Through the medium of prayer, God's will becomes apparent to man. It is a means not as much for the purpose of changing God's will as of raising us to a spiritual level where we can see eye to eye with God.

KINDS OF PRAYER.—As we mentioned previously, there are three kinds of prayer. The first of these is the prayer of praise.[2] Praise is an expression of love. It asks for nothing, neither does it thank, even though the heart is filled with the emotion of gratitude. A son may throw his arms around his father and say, "Dad, I think you are a good scout." That is praise expressed by the son. If this does not happen very often it may cause the father to become skeptical and say, "You must want something, son."

But God is not skeptical and there are times in every Christian's life when he just wants to praise God for His goodness and mercy. This type of prayer is expressed only by those individuals who are in fellowship with God. There were times in the Psalmist's life when God became so real to him that, spiritually speaking, he put his arms around the Almighty and said, "Bless the Lord, O my soul. O Lord my God, thou art very great: thou art clothed with honor and majesty." [3] There are no ulterior motives in true praise. It is an expression of love. You will notice that the Lord's Prayer concludes with praise: "For Thine is the kingdom and the power and the glory, forever. Amen."

This emotion, praise, is also expressed in many of the responses that are sung by Christians, such as: "Glory be to

[2] Psalms 103:1-5.   [3] Psalms 104:1.

the Father, and to the Son, and to the Holy Ghost; As it was in the beginning, is now, and ever shall be, world without end. Amen." Or: "Praise God from whom all blessings flow; Praise Him, all creatures here below; Praise Him above, ye heavenly host: Praise Father, Son, and Holy Ghost. Amen."

Praise is also expressed in our lives by the way we live. A person cannot avoid reflecting it in his personality when fellowship has been disrupted with any of his intimate friends. It is also true that the Christian reflects it in his personality when a strained relationship exists between him and God. When he is in the harmony of fellowship, praise expresses itself in his attitude toward life, toward his fellow man, and toward the problems he meets daily.

The second type of prayer is that of thanksgiving.[4] Thanksgiving is a courteous thing, to say the least. When anyone does anything for us that we appreciate it is natural and courteous to say, "Thank you." However, because we are inherently so selfish, there are many times that we forget to express our thanks. Once Jesus healed ten men of that dreaded disease, leprosy.[5] Only one took the time to come back and thank him. Jesus was amazed at this thoughtlessness and expressed it when He said, "Were not the ten cleansed? But where are the nine?"

Thanksgiving implies that we recognize that we have received something for which we should be thankful. The bounty of God has become a reality for the thankful person. This does not necessarily mean that he has been fortunate enough to realize unusual financial or other material gain. Every Christian has plenty to be thankful for all the time. The possibility of forgiveness of sins, salvation, and eternal life are gifts so precious that the Christian can well feel grateful toward God any time he thinks of Him.

[4] Psalms 92:1; Ephesians 5:20.   [5] Luke 17:11-19.

The third type of prayer is that of petition, or asking for things. The Lord invites us to bring to Him whatsoever is upon the heart and the mind.[6]

In the Lord's Prayer [7] Jesus teaches us to ask God for that which is necessary for body and soul. Three of these petitions direct our thoughts Godward: 1. "Hallowed be Thy name," 2. "Thy kingdom come," 3. "Thy will be done in earth as it is in heaven." The last four petitions direct our thoughts manward: 1. "Give us this day our daily bread," 2. "And forgive us our debts as we forgive our debtors," 3. "And lead us not into temptation," 4. "But deliver us from evil." In these petitions we ask God about those things that are essential. Even the physical is taken into consideration when we pray for our "daily bread." These petitions recognize God as the source of all things material and spiritual. Since He is that source, it is wise for man to talk over with Him whatever he thinks he needs. The answer will be according to God's wisdom.

FORMS OF PRAYER.—Some certain form or attitude is considered by many to be essential in the act of prayer. Even the forms of language are sometimes thought of as important, and for that reason many unconsciously adopt the use of the "thees" and "thous" and the "hasts" and "dosts" when they pray. The inability to use such formal phrasings does deter many persons from praying in the presence of others. There are those who pray standing up, some sitting down, others kneeling, with a bowed head, closed eyes, or folded hands. They feel that one or a combination of these forms is essential, or they have been taught from childhood that a specific way is the way to pray.

Jesus gives no instruction as to outward form or mode. It is left with the individual to learn how he can best con-

[6] Matthew 7:7; 21:22.   [7] Matthew 6:9–13.

centrate his thoughts and express his feelings toward God. In this respect perhaps the only essential is sincerity. Since God knows our thoughts He will pay little attention to whether we are standing or sitting.[8] This statement may seem rather flippant to some who think that sitting in the presence of the Almighty is an act of disrespect. However, an attitude of respect can be expressed if it is in the heart, no matter what the posture of the individual may be. Kneeling seems to be regarded as expressing more sincerity. Tradition tells us that when they tried to coffin James they found his knees so calloused that they could not be made straight. He was nicknamed "Camel Knees" and we are told that his knees grew that way because he was upon them so much in prayer. It is true that the act of kneeling does something to an individual who is accustomed to it. It does express deep humility. On the other hand, that same humility can be expressed in other ways also. So as far as the form of prayer is concerned, it can be said that the important thing is the mental and spiritual attitude of the worshiper.

Prayer may be spoken aloud or it may be thought. It does not necessarily have to be long. However, prayers can also be so short that they are hardly an act of fellowship. Prayers may be public or private. Those who lead in public prayer do not necessarily have to inform God about everything that is going on, merely to consume time. The leader should think himself into the mood of those whose prayer he is expressing. He should bring to God those things that are important for those who are joining him in this prayer. Again we say that the efficacy of public praying does not consist in many words.[9] There is a danger that "double-action prayers" may pray us into Heaven and back out again.

Various denominations emphasize or teach modes and forms of prayer. These are offered as aids in the act, not as

[8] Psalms 139:1–6.   [9] Matthew 6:7.

essentials to the act. They become so much a part of the religious life that when the praying one assumes this form or posture a certain attitude is produced. Other aids, such as the Rosary and the prayer book, are used by some churches. There are those who believe that certain memorized prayers have special significance. All in all, we can say that if any of these forms aid the individual in forming an attitude of prayer, then they are efficacious.

THE EMOTIONS IN PRAYER.—The emotions are as much a part of our makeup as are reason, imagination, or memory. There is nothing about the emotions that we should be ashamed of, if they are purposefully directed and properly controlled. Man lives by his emotions as well as by bread, and they are a vital part of his reflexes and other organic functions. They are a part of the total personality and must be taken into consideration when we consider any important phase of living.

The emotions play an important role in the act of prayer. Such emotions as love, hatred, jealousy, persistence, kindness, praise, gratitude, forgiveness, a spirit of sacrifice, faith, and deep devotion, all are used in praying. When we think of persistence, for example, it reminds us of the man who knocked at midnight.[10] This man came to his neighbor's door and knocked. Even though the neighbor heard him, he did not get up. He did not want to be bothered at midnight. But this man was in desperate circumstances. Guests had come to his home. They were hungry; they must have bread. Had this man left after the first attempt to arouse his neighbor he would not have received the bread. We can imagine him there in the dark watching the door intently, looking for a gleam of light from within. Again he knocked and louder this time. He will stay with it until this neighbor does meet his needs

[10] Luke 11:5–13.

and he will knock so loudly that he will awaken the children also. This man means business! Because he is so persistent the neighbor does arise and gives him more than he asked for.

Sometimes God seems to be like this sleepy neighbor. We think He should rush to our aid immediately, and our impatience makes Him seem that way. (We forget that on many occasions He had good reasons to become impatient with us.) In this parable, Jesus did not mean that God is sleepy, but that we should seek spiritual blessings as persistently as we seek material ones.

Resignation to the will of God is also important in praying.[11] In one Scripture reference, a widow came to the judge for justice. He did not listen to her. Evidently she was so poor that she had no bribe to offer. She came again and again. She was confident that eventually justice would be meted out to her, and her confidence was rewarded. There are times in life when we come upon situations that baffle us and cause us to question God's justice. He may even seem to be an unjust judge who does not hear us when we pray. If we have the confidence and are willing to submit ourselves to God's holy will and continue in prayer regardless of how things seem to be, He will answer us even beyond our greatest expectations.

The element of forgiveness is also essential in prayer.[12] In the Lord's Prayer we pray that God will forgive us in proportion to our willingness to forgive others who have sinned against us. In the very act of forgiving others, we raise ourselves to the level of fellowship with Him. Any approach to God must be clean enough to come near Him. If we bring a sacrifice, either material or spiritual, the sacrifice is tainted unless our attitude toward our fellow men is the attitude that we would like God to have toward us. For many, this is one of the most difficult of all the Christian

[11] Luke 18:2-8.   [12] Matthew 6:14, 15.

virtues. But it is the sign that distinguishes the Christian. If the worshiper is going to be like the pagan in his attitudes, then why be a Christian? This was hard for the disciples also. Peter thought that forgiving seven times was stretching things quite a bit. Jesus' reply, suggesting even seventy times seven, does not mean that we can count out four hundred ninety instances of forgiveness and stop there; instead, Jesus indicates an attitude of forgiveness that is a way of living.

In the parable of the debtor recorded in Matthew 18, we see ourselves in relation to God. What an enormous debt we owe Him! How much He has done for us and continues to do in extending the gift of salvation! It does seem rather small on our part to expect God to cancel this enormous debt and then, in turn, not be willing to forget a very small amount that a fellow man owes us. Forgiveness is one of the great emotions that is exercised in prayer.

Faith is another essential element. The story is told of the good old lady who had a fir tree in her front yard. She tried unsuccessfully to get someone to remove it. She heard her pastor preach about the power of prayer and decided to try that. Before she went to sleep that night she asked God to remove the tree. On rising the next morning she hastened to the front window; looking out she muttered, "Humm—, I thought so!" There may have been many reasons why the tree still stood, but in the first place she did not believe what she was praying for.

That faith is important in prayer is emphasized by Jesus.[13] However, we should not confuse faith with trying God's patience, as was done by a rural mail carrier and his wife. A day or so after they had left on a summer vacation, the neighbors heard their horse kicking and neighing in the barn. They investigated and found that the animal had been left without food or water. When the returning vacationers were

[13] Matthew 21:22.

confronted with this negligence they replied that they had prayed over the matter before leaving and were confident that God would see to it that the animal was taken care of. You may say that He did, and perhaps that is true; but it is also trying God's patience, and the element of irresponsibility is more prominent in this instance than faith.

Faith has important subjective values. If we are confident that God will hear and answer our prayers we will leave no stone unturned in cooperating with Him. This gives us confidence also that things work out for the best. We must trust God and believe that He will answer our sincere prayers either in the way that we expect Him to answer or in the way that He deems best.

Anger is also an emotion that may be exercised in prayer. You may think that this is an unusual emotion to be brought into play in this sacred act. We must bear in mind that all anger is not sinful.[14] As a matter of fact, some persons hardly do anything constructive until angry. There is an anger that is righteous and an anger that is not. There are some things that Christian people should not tolerate because they are contrary to the will of God. To accept such things complacently is nothing less than being so good that one is good for nothing. There is a time to be angry and there is a time not to be angry. When Lord Wilberforce realized the many evils growing out of the slave traffic, he became so angry that he thoroughly hated the practice. This righteous anger caused him to devote his life to the abolishment of this scourge in England. The same thing is true of Abraham Lincoln in our own country. When as a young man he saw a slave auction in New Orleans, he was so outraged that he made it one of the great aims of his life to fight this sin. Such anger and hatred are not sinful, but akin to the righteous indignation of God toward those things and practices that

[14] Ephesians 4:26.

would deprive mankind of its heritage. It is true that sometimes the Psalmist became quite personal in his hatred
toward his enemies.[15] This attitude, however, should have
no part in a Christian's prayer unless he has in his heart a
sincere desire that his enemies may change and live. To ask
God to destroy or subdue enemies for our sake is certainly
very selfish and unworthy of a follower of Christ. But to
hate those things which make enemies is another matter.
Selfishness, greed, inconsiderateness, all are things that men
could very well live without. When the Christian sees these
sins robbing men of their birthright he cannot be complacent.
He can become a crusader in his prayers and as a result he
will do what he can to remove these sins and still keep fellowship with his fellow men. In other words, he will pray, not
that his enemies be stricken or destroyed, but rather that they
be changed from their evil ways.

When a person becomes thoroughly aroused it is well for
him to weigh the matter very carefully. When he is quite
certain that there are justifiable grounds for his anger, he
may pray over the matter. Through prayer the emotion of
anger will be transformed into a quiet determination to
eliminate the causes of his anger. It is understood that the
Christian will never hate any person.[16] But he does have the
right to pray that the evils which plague individuals and
society may be undone. Among such evils are war, poverty,
class and race distinction, social pride, and spiritual arrogance.

Another emotion that is primary in the act of prayer is that
of love. This love is Godward on the part of man and manward on the part of God. As far as man is concerned, his
love for God is bound to find expression in prayer because
we cannot help confiding in those whom we love. The act of
prayer is the expression of this love for God. It indicates that
the individual is in personal relationship with his Father.

[15] Psalms 44:5–6.   [16] Matthew 5:44.

Jesus was so closely united with the Father that He often withdrew to be alone with God in prayer. He constantly felt the presence of His Father. He did not always have to assume a certain position or express His thoughts in order to be praying. His life is an expression of fellowship with God. This fellowship, or communion, is what the Apostle means when he says to "pray without ceasing." [17]

Love in prayer also draws man manward. It causes him to realize his oneness with the whole family of the human race. Under the Father we are all brothers and sisters. As members of one family we are certainly interested in the welfare of one another. Then when we pray for our fellow men we establish our kinship.

Pity and humility are other emotions brought into play in the act of prayer. Prayer also is a stimulator of man's mental and spiritual faculties. Among the mental and spiritual faculties so exercised are memory, reason, and imagination. The Christian could no more abstain from the practice of prayer than he could from eating. It is the food and the exercise of his soul.

B. What Does Prayer Do?

Since we have studied the kinds, the forms, and the emotions of prayer, it is well for us to consider what prayer does. Many books have been written on this subject because it is so important. And in answer to the question "What does prayer do?" there are about as many and varied replies as there are persons who have reflected upon the question. All the answers may be considered under two general headings: subjective values and objective values.

SUBJECTIVE VALUES OF PRAYER.—Since the soul, the mind, and the body are the three factors of the total person-

[17] I Thessalonians 5:17.

ality, the act of prayer has its effect upon all three of them. Just as in the matter of health it is impossible to draw a clear line dividing the influence of these three factors, so in considering the subjective values of prayer it will be impossible clearly to divide these three factors of personality. As the attempt is made and we consider them separately it must also be borne in mind that all three are interrelated.

Prayer lifts the soul into the presence of God. Here for example is an individual who is sorely tempted. He must make a choice and in the conflict he resorts to prayer. While he is praying the spirit of God leads him to a decision. The decision he makes is more in accord with what is right than it would have been had he not prayed. While he prays the distinction between right and wrong becomes clearer. As far as ethics is concerned, there is but one choice to make. Now that the choice is clear, the temptation recedes and he can follow this course of action. Once he has made his decision a sense of calmness comes over him. His soul has been raised until it sees on the level with God and since God is its natural element, peace is the natural result.

Prayer also is the remedy that will heal a guilt stress. Once the source of the guilt is talked over with God in confession, the uneasiness begins to leave. As long as the guilt stress is present the individual is nervous in the inner man; this nervousness may drive him to various perversions in a futile attempt to get rid of it and find peace. There are those who resort to drugs or alcohol in the vain hope that these will help them forget. In this manner the guilt stress may be diverted for the time being. The individual fools himself into believing that he has gotten rid of it. However, once the effects have worn off the stress becomes deeper and more urgent.

The expression of a guilt stress may also be perverted into a desire for superficial excitement and entertainment.

Under the influence of such stimuli, mental and physical hyperactivity concentrates the attention to such an extent that the guilt stress is sidetracked for the duration of the excitement or the entertainment. But mental and physical excitements have their limitations. They must end sooner or later and the old guilt stress then reappears.

Under such conditions, when the individual turns to prayer rather than to any other artificial means he is resorting to the natural activity of the soul. It can be compared to the physical in this way: let us say a man is suffering with a stomach disorder. He can either take orally certain medicines that will help his stomach digest the food, or take certain medicines that will correct the disorder. If he resorts to the former, as soon as he discontinues his medicine the old disorder disturbs him again. Prayer is the medicine that corrects the disorder of the soul.

Prayer causes man to assume his royal office.[18] As a potential child of God man has royal blood in his veins. He exercises his office when he has a conference with the King. In the act of prayer, verily he walks into the palace unchallenged. He is a child of the King and has the privilege of His presence. He may take his place beside the throne and talk confidentially with the King. As a matter of fact, he may talk with the King on equal terms.[19] The King does not reason with a servant or a slave. The one who prays does not even have to be subservient; when he sits beside the throne he is the prince of the land.[20] The King invites him to express himself in complete confidence, fully and without reserve. He may even insist in his prayer to such an extent that he can command the King.

In this we see the tremendous potentialities of prayer. The great power of a praying person is evident. In these con-

[18] I Peter 2:9.
[19] Isaiah 1:18.
[20] Isaiah 45:11.

versations in the throne room, things of great or minor importance are talked over and decided. A man who may seem to be quite inconsequential as far as his power upon others is concerned exercises a great office when he prays. We must bear in mind, however, that such a person is to be trusted. One who is on intimate terms with the King is neither vindictive nor arrogant. Were he so he would never get near enough to whisper into the King's ear. Through prayer he makes himself fit for the office of royal priest. It is a royalty that is not acquired either through heredity or bequest, but a royalty that is merited through achievement and sincerity.

In the act of prayer man becomes his own priest. In the Old Testament it was necessary for the worshiper to approach God through some especially designated person, a person of the priesthood. Through special training and family connections certain individuals were fitted for this office. It was necessary for them to be of the House of Levi and only descendants of this son of Jacob were set apart for this special religious service. Once the great, all-sufficient sacrifice was made on Calvary, Jesus Christ became the eternal High Priest [21] and every individual became a potential royal priest who may approach the Almighty through Jesus Christ. The priesthood of all believers is one of the great doctrines emphasized in the Reformation and held by all Protestants today. In essence it means that there is no mediator between man and God other than Jesus Christ. When the individual prays he exercises his office of priesthood and can himself come into the presence of the King.

Prayer also influences the mind. It clears the thinking, removes the muddle, and makes the issues at hand straighten out clearly. Here is a man praying over a problem that puzzles him. As he engages in prayer, other things that would enter

[21] Hebrews 8:1–13.

into his mind to distract his attention are closed out. His interest is centered on finding a solution. As things become clearer, because the elements that would prejudice him are excluded as far as it is possible for a human to exclude them, the decision that is made is the best decision of which he is capable. We do not say that this decision is always right, but we do say that prayer will help him more than anything else to make the right decision. This assumes that he is relatively honest with himself and that his intentions toward others are not selfish. If the decision to be made is of special importance it is well, after he has considered the arguments on both sides, to talk the matter over with God in seclusion. He does his best and his clearest thinking in this way.

Prayer also rests the mind of the person who is harried with a busy life and finds himself concerned with so many other things that he is nervously restless. If it is at all possible for him to take a little time out for quiet prayer he will find that it will rest him mentally.

Another subjective mental value of prayer lies in its motivation of the will. Motives are not inherited. They are ideals that we acquire. These ideals become the drives of the will. Just how high these ideals will be depends upon the individual's cultural environment as it has been tempered by his past experiences. If he has trained his soul in ethical living, his goals of aspiration are high. The measure of achieving these ethical goals will depend upon the power of his will.

In the very act of prayer man raises the level of his aspiration. In talking with God, the spirit of God motivates his thinking. He is no longer satisfied with living in the mire. He sees very clearly the choice that he must make as a follower of Christ. The Christian way becomes a goal of achievement. With such motivation he lives on a much higher plane than he did without the exercise of prayer.

Prayer expresses itself also in service. He is no longer satisfied with just thinking about things or talking about what ought to be done. He himself has to have a part in this achievement.[22] The whole emphasis of the Gospel lies in the direction of doing the will of God. Christianity is not a matter of philosophizing, but rather an expression of the ideals inculcated by the spirit of Jesus. For that reason our religion is dynamic. No person can be truly religious and not do anything about it. A man cannot be a follower of Christ and be unconcerned about the welfare of his fellow men. Prayer is the impetus that motivates him to action and for that reason it is vital to the realization of the Kingdom of God.

Prayer has its subjective values, not only for the soul and mind, but also for the body. While our investigations in this field are yet very much in their infancy, those who deal with the sick have come to realize that prayer has a definite therapeutic value. The developments in the field of psychosomatic medicine definitely prove that the mind and the soul have their effects upon the physical functions of the body. The primary stresses in illness—fear, guilt, pain, and loneliness—affect the functions of the body through the influence of the endocrine glands and the cerebrospinal nervous system.

Let us take for example the element of faith. It is commonly understood that a patient's confidence in his physician helps him recover because it relieves his mind of anxiety stresses. This confidence gives him the assurance that he will get well. The absence of restlessness, worry, and uncertainty causes him to sleep better and to enjoy his food, thus aiding both digestion and assimilation.

On a much higher scale, the same thing is true concerning faith in God. The patient with a strong faith in God, other factors being equal, stands a much better chance of recovering from an illness than a patient who does not have faith. We

[22] Matthew 7:21; James 2:17.

can readily see why a strong faith in God would remove worry, concern, and uncertainty. When there are doubts, he prays, and prayer brings him the reassurance he needs.

The fellowship with God helps to quell the fears that so often plague us, especially when we face a crisis in life. The normal individual is bound to be apprehensive when he faces an operation, or an amputation, or a long convalescence, or death. Through the medium of prayer he may have fellowship with God, who is the source of all life. The words of Scripture,[23] "And we know that all things work together for good to them that love God," become the reassurance that eliminates fear. Through confidence he becomes at ease and resigns himself to that which will be God's will for him. In cooperation with God he will do his very best to aid the processes of healing by not worrying about them. He will accept the outcome with a stoical spirit and make the best of it, even if he knows that he will not recover. Through his faith he knows that death is the transition to eternal life.

When there is a guilt stress present in illness, prayer has its value in that through its medium confession is made, and through confession the stress is relieved. It is understood that a guilt stress has its effects upon the physical processes also. Thus, prayer has the subjective value of relieving and of promoting the healing processes.

Prayer is both introvertive and extrovertive; introvertive in that it causes the individual to examine his spiritual state, extrovertive in that it expresses concern about others. The extrovertive element in prayer has therapeutic value in that it directs the thoughts from self to others. The praying person rises out of selfish interests and centers his attention upon something outside himself. Thus becoming interested in the welfare of others he raises his achievement levels. The drive

[23] Romans 8:28.

to do something about it becomes more acute and he is benefited spiritually, mentally, and physically.

OBJECTIVE VALUES.—All these things that we have mentioned are the upward drive of prayer. They lift man higher. But prayer also has its objective values. We often hear it said that "prayer changes things," and it certainly does. Just how much the will of God is changed by prayer is not for us to say, and there are those who contend that the will of God is never changed by prayer but, through its means, man conforms to God's will. This statement may occasion much controversy. The thought behind it has been debated through the centuries and it is not for us to settle it here. But whether it makes man conform to God's will or changes God's will for man, we do know that it does have results. Man can do things when he prays that he could not otherwise do.

Many benevolent institutions have been supported through prayer on the part of those who are interested. People tell us that they feel the influence of prayer on their lives. The saints of the past have always solicited prayer. In Scripture the Apostle Paul says, "Brethren, pray for us."

Because there are so many things about the spiritual world that we do not yet understand, we do not want to set a hard and fast rule and say that prayer does not change God's will toward man. On the other hand we would not want to think of God as an individual who cannot make up His mind and is persuaded by us to change a decision He has made. The spirit of God is too great, good, and purposive to depend upon our limited intelligence and spirituality. But that the prayers of the faithful have something to do in directing the destinies of men is commonly believed by Christian people. The Roman Catholic Church has built its purgatory structure upon the presumption that praying people can influence the condition of the soul in the eternal life. But it can also be said that whatever happens to that soul through the influence of prayer is foreordained of God and according to His will. So the argument resembles a circle. But the objective results of prayer have been so manifest that whatever the arguments may be, Christian people will continue to pray—and as they pray they will work. It must also be borne in mind that when people know that they are being remembered in prayer, this awareness will influence them.

To summarize then, we may say that prayer is man's greatest privilege. He does not know his possibilities until he becomes a praying man.

For Discussion

1. What is prayer?
2. Discuss the three kinds of prayer. Which kind of prayer is used most often? How are these expressed in the Lord's Prayer?
3. How may forms help in the act of prayer? Do you think forms in prayer are important? What form do you assume in praying?
4. Discuss the role of the emotions in the act of prayer. Do you think life would be dull without emotions? Should the emotions be suppressed?
5. How may prayer serve as a healthful expression of the emotions? Of reason? Of creative imagination?
6. How may prayer become a spiritually cleansing force?
7. Discuss answers to prayer that have come to your attention.
8. What does prayer do for the person who is praying?
9. Do you know what is meant by the expression, "the priesthood of all believers"?
10. How may prayer motivate the praying person? What does it have to do with goals of achievement?
11. What are some specific objective values in prayer?

CHAPTER 8

What About the Life to Come?

One who never turned his back but
> marched breast forward,
> Never doubted clouds would break,
> Never dreamed, though right were worsted,
>> wrong would triumph,
> Held we fall to rise, are baffled to
>> fight better,
> Sleep to wake.

No, at noonday in the bustle of
> man's worktime
> Greet the unseen with a cheer!
> Bid him forward, breast and back
>> as either should be,
> "Strive and thrive!" Cry, "Speed—
>> fight on, fare ever
> There as here!"

ROBERT BROWNING *

Ability to see the consequences of acts is a mark of intelligence. Some consequences are immediate and some consequences are more remote. Often the more important are the more remote. It is therefore a mark of greater wisdom to see the more remote consequences. A person is not likely to jump in front of a moving train, for evil consequences will immediately follow, but he may do something to ruin his health since the consequences of these actions are often delayed. If, however, he saw vividly these more remote consequences he would not commit the act. If a person is intelligent and knows certainly that certain deeds will result in eter-

* Quoted by permission of and arrangement with Houghton Mifflin Co., authorized publishers.

nal pain or eternal death he will not commit these acts. It is therefore with a sense of their practical value that we turn to these thoughts about the life to come.

A. Is This Life a Preparation?

There are still some persons who conclude a prayer or a grace at table with the petition "In heaven save us for Christ's sake." The life in this world is something to be lived through in order to get to the next one. During the Middle Ages the earth was thought to be a place of preparation for heaven and every Christian a candidate for a place of blessedness when the earthly life is finished. The tasks of life were meant to be done and the trials and tribulations of this present life to be endured because of their value as a preparation for the life to come. Even today some denominations and sects emphasize the life to come, where inequalities will be erased. With the mind turned to the future, a person more easily endures the present.

When one thinks of this life only as a preparation for eternity, he tends not to try to better conditions here, especially social and economic conditions. To do so would imply disloyalty to God by refusing to accept the discipline of unfortunate circumstances. This may be one reason why the people of medieval Europe were so poor. India of today, with its widespread poverty and its apparent indifference to human suffering and human need, suggests to us what may happen when a whole society turns its face to what lies beyond the grave.

This view also has a tendency to deny an interest in the world of nature. In the Middle Ages science was stifled. When some individuals were determined to learn about the world of nature they were permitted to study Aristotle, a great scientist of ancient times. But the science of Aristotle was in books, and men showed an increasing interest in the actualities of the world about them. When interest in science finally won the day medieval other-worldliness gave way to modern this-worldliness.

GROWING INTEREST IN THIS WORLD.—Along with interest in the world of nature came interest in the earth as the home of man, and in man himself. This interest in man, which has been called humanism, was another force pulling away from the other-worldliness of medieval times.

Today in the lands roughly designated as Christendom, the tendency is to be impatient of waiting till after death for the blessed life to begin. To ask people to work only for immortality seems like asking them to give up their rights now for a chance to "eat pie in the sky by and by." The developing humanism of modern times has given rise to rapid social change brought about because of the desire for better conditions in this world now. Great philanthropists have given large fortunes to better social and economic conditions. Some have devoted their entire lives to reforms that would remove conditions which bring suffering to underprivileged humanity.

LOSSES DUE TO CHANGE OF ATTITUDE.—While we recognize the benefits resulting from this movement away from extreme other-worldliness, yet we realize that there have been important accompanying losses.

(1) Attention focused upon the blessings of the present life leads to a feverish search for immediate and material blessings. There has been a restless discontent. Discontent can be very helpful when one is dissatisfied with conditions which he can improve. But discontent can be very harmful when it leads a person restlessly from one activity to another as each in turn fails to bring satisfaction.

The extreme interest in the immediate and material has shown itself mainly in a desire for physical comfort, along with an accumulation of goods. An accumulation of goods calls for fierce competition. We see people trying to keep up with the Joneses, with many wanting to be the Joneses. Since it is impossible for everyone to have exactly the same amount there is a constant struggle, which is fruitless and futile. This leads to internal strife and international conflict. Strikes and wars are symptoms of this deadly rivalry for material possessions. Not only do strikes and wars furnish patients for nurses and doctors, but so does the sense of futility and frustration. Deeply felt needs go unsatisfied. The mind is divided within itself.

(2) The retreat from other-worldliness has also resulted in the lack of confidence in the eternal values. Many of the movements benefiting mankind have taken generations to achieve. A roll of the heroes of history would include the names of many martyrs whose causes eventually triumphed. Jeremiah, Socrates, Jesus, John Huss, and Lincoln were among those who died before their causes were won. Under the spell of immediate interest in material things, men lose interest in these great processes which take centuries. That is what led one college president to say that our modern madness is the mania for immediacy.

(3) Men lose, furthermore, the poise and power which one feels when he realizes that, though personally defeated, he may win in a larger sense because his acts are in harmony with the purpose of God. There are a few who can sponsor great causes even though they cannot see any opportunity to participate in their final triumph, but it takes a noble soul to make such a sacrifice. For the majority of mankind long-term objectives give way to immediate half-measures. When a group of men were discussing what might be done to accomplish a lasting and stable international order, the remark of one of the men, a professed Christian, was rather typical, "I do not care what happens twenty-five years from now. I want to live now."

ALL THIS AND HEAVEN TOO.—The Christian view of immortality does not compel a person to make a choice between the present life and the life beyond the body's death. This life is a preparation for the next in the same way that today is a preparation for tomorrow, and tomorrow a preparation for the next day. Each day a person lives as well as prepares. He may begin to live the eternal life now. That means that eternal life has a quality—depth and breadth as well as length.[1] There is no value in mere endless existence. Some loafers we may know would probably not want to live forever; as Professor Brightman says, "The eternal life is a life worthy of being eternal."

B. How Can We Believe in Immortality?

THE RESURRECTION OF JESUS.—The Christian believes that since Jesus arose from the dead, therefore those who follow after Him will rise from the dead. This is the faith that Saint Paul expressed in his great chapter on the resurrection.[2] This is the faith that Jesus lived. He was almost certain that He faced death in Jerusalem.[3] Yet He looked confidently ahead to victory. He told the Disciples that the next meal He would have with them would be in His Father's Kingdom.[4] He seemed to be thinking of a eucharist celebrating the victory when the Kingdom for which He was about to die becomes a reality.

The Sadducees, who did not believe in the resurrection, asked Jesus specifically about His belief. They used the time-worn gag about the woman who had married seven brothers in succession because each had died childless.[5] They were sure that eternal life would make her a polygamist. Jesus'

---

[1] John 17:3.
[2] I Corinthians 15.
[3] Luke 13:33.
[4] Matthew 26:29. See also Mark 14:25 and Luke 22:18.
[5] Matthew 22:28.

reply indicates that in the first place there would be no marriage in heaven and that disposed of the moral problem. Jesus seems to believe that it is not a physical existence.

Secondly, he used the rabbinical method so familiar to them to show them that the founders of their nation still lived. God told Moses that He was the God of Abraham, Isaac, and Jacob.[6] Since He is not the God of the dead these patriarchs must still be alive. Though we may not follow this reasoning, yet we do see that Jesus believed in immortality.

DIFFICULTIES IN THINKING OF IMMORTALITY.—There are some difficulties in the way of thinking of the immortality or the survival of the spiritual nature.

(1) In the first place we have never experienced consciousness apart from the body. But that difficulty is not necessarily insurmountable. For that matter we have never experienced a lump of earth suspended in space without material support, but we no longer believe that the earth rests upon the backs of four elephants.

(2) The reverse of this difficulty is that consciousness seems to be dependent upon the brain and nerve cells. Our difficulty at this point depends upon our view of consciousness. Of course, if consciousness is a product of the brain and the nerve cells there seems to be no possibility of the survival of the soul. One may, however, believe that the body is an instrument of the mind—that the body is the channel through which consciousness flows. That is the view held by some of the great thinkers.[7] The mind exerts so much control over the neural and other bodily processes as to indicate that it is no mere product of the brain. In forms of religious ex-

[6] Exodus 3:15.
[7] See William James, J. S. Haldane, Henri Bergson, and William Mac-Dougall in W. K. Wright, *A Student's Philosophy of Religion*, The Macmillan Co., 1935, pages 433–442.

perience, for example conversion, it seems that a power from without comes into one's life. The loss or impairment of consciousness that follows brain injury is often followed after an interval by the restoration of the lost functions. The mind seems to have found new and uninjured portions of the brain to use for these activities.

REASONS FOR BELIEF IN IMMORTALITY.—We have already seen that Christians believe in human immortality because Jesus arose from the dead. Many think that this belief is supported by philosophical arguments, which are simply the processes by which a person thinks things through. It is like checking your answer to an arithmetic problem to be sure you are right. While there are many such arguments, the following seem to be the strongest.

(1) The argument from duty. A moral universe demands perfect obedience to duty. When a man's duty has been accomplished he always sees other things ahead that he should do. If the demands of duty are to have meaning, there must always be further opportunity for its achievement. That further opportunity calls for an eternity in which all man's duties may be done.

(2) The argument from justice. In a just or moral universe there would be a union of happiness and virtue. This is a just universe. Though many times we see injustice, the needs of justice are served in this life more than they fail to be realized. The sense of justice in human beings responds to a justice inherent in the nature of things, just as a person's appetite responds to the presence of food. Yet the perfect union of happiness and virtue is not attained upon the earth. Many persons undeservingly are frustrated or suffer pain. On the other hand, many seem to fail to reap the results of their misdeeds. Therefrom arises the belief that the personality survives the body. Just as justice is attained in the

long run better than over a short period of time, so it is attained better in eternity than in time.

(3) The argument from emergent evolution. This argument grows out of the study of the history of the universe. Those who have examined the evidence for purpose in the universe tell us that the universe seems to be moving toward some end or goal. In the physical phases the development has been toward life. In the biological history the development has been toward the creation of the human being. In the spiritual phases the trend has been toward the goal of the highest development of personality—the enlightenment of reason—the increase and conservation of values. With such a view, it is difficult to see how the thing of greatest value in the world should be temporal and the material things eternal.

(4) Argument from the presence of evil. Evil considered by itself has no meaning. Many persons die in the midst of poverty and suffering and failure. One can see how evil in the sense of suffering might be helpful if the sufferer could learn a lesson from it. But if there is no life beyond physical death many persons will never have the opportunity to benefit from this discipline.

(5) Argument from the character of God. Some believe that God can be judged by the same moral standards which Christ held up for human beings.[8] He must therefore treat human beings as of supreme value. Only personal immortality is compatible with treating persons as of supreme value. To raise hopes that are to be shattered, to give capacities that are never to be developed, to inspire a love for others who are to be destroyed, are not the deeds of one who is good. "If there be a God, man's immortality is certain."[9]

[8] Matthew 5:48.
[9] E. S. Brightman, *An Introduction to Philosophy*, Henry Holt & Co., 1935, page 349.

C. Punishment and Reward

It is very difficult to tell what is going to happen tomorrow, and the person who attempts to find out what will take place in the life beyond the grave is in real difficulties. Whenever one thinks of the survival of the soul he tries to think what life in the world to come will be like. Usually a person thinks that those who have lived rightly will be much happier than those who have done wrong.[10]

EARLY CHRISTIAN THOUGHT.—It may surprise some of our readers to know that the early Christians believed that eternal life would be upon the earth. For two centuries after the disciples last saw Jesus on the Mount of Olives, the church fully expected that He would come again in the flesh and set up an earthly kingdom,[11] and that those who had died would arise again and join Him in that Kingdom.[12] After many years a large number of the early Christians began to think they would not live until His return.[13] Some even thought of His coming as a spiritual event.[14] Gradually Christians began to believe that they would go to live with Jesus in heaven.[15]

HEAVEN, PURGATORY, AND HELL.—In Christian theology there was developed a view of heaven to which the righteous would go to live eternally in the presence of God, and of hell where those who disobeyed the will of God would be punished forever. There are Biblical passages upon which such a view can be based. There was developed also the doctrine of purgatory. According to this belief all those who were neither perfectly good nor hopelessly bad enter an intermediate realm

[10] II Chronicles 6:30; Psalms 62:12; Proverbs 24:12; Matthew 16:27; Romans 2:6; Galatians 6:7.
[11] Acts 1:6-11.
[12] I Thessalonians 4:15-17.   [14] John 14:2, 3, 18, 19.
[13] Philippians 1:23-24.   [15] John 14:3.

where they suffer the consequences of their sins and are prepared for the heavenly life. While in purgatory they can be helped by the prayers of the living.[16]

The doctrine of purgatory has certain things to recommend it. In the first place it makes provision for those who are neither so wicked that they should be eternally punished nor yet good enough to go immediately to eternal bliss. A teacher soon learns that his students should be divided into approximately three classes: those who are brilliant, those who are failures, and those who are average. A glimpse of society about us would indicate that morally people should be divided into the same three classes. This doctrine makes provision for the average between the two extremes. In the second place, it establishes a bond between the living and the dead and makes the future life more vivid in our minds. On the other hand, the doctrine lays itself open to certain abuses. Superstitions have arisen; and harmful practices, such as the sale of indulgences, have grown up because of the support furnished by this doctrine. The Reformation, both within the church and under the Protestants, was largely a protest against these abuses. The Catholic Church removed the abuses and retained the doctrine of purgatory. The Protestants substituted the doctrine of instant sanctification of the saved at death.

[16] For the Biblical basis of this doctrine let us quote from the revision of Challoner—Rheims version in 1941, "Whoever speaks a word against the Son of Man, it shall be forgiven him; but whoever speaks against the Holy Spirit, it will not be forgiven him, either in this world or in the world to come." (Matthew 12:32) "Come to terms with thy opponent quickly while thou art with him on the way; lest thy opponent deliver thee to the judge and the judge to the officer, and thou be cast into prison. Amen I say to thee, thou wilt not come out from it until thou hast paid the last penny." (Matthew 5:25–26) "And making a gathering, he sent 12,000 drachmas of silver to Jerusalem for sacrifice to the offering for the sins of the dead thinking well and religiously concerning the resurrection (for if he had not hoped that they that were slain should rise again, it would have seemed superfluous and vain to pray for the dead). And because he considered that they who had fallen asleep with godliness, had great grace laid up for them. It is therefore a holy and wholesome thing to pray for the dead, that they may be released from sins." (II Maccabees 12:43–46)

INSTANT SANCTIFICATION OF THE SAVED.—The saved, who according to the Protestant view are sanctified at death, are thought of as those who have accepted Christ in this life. No matter how they have lived, those who accept Christ, even at death's door, enter into the eternal life wholly cleansed from their sins.

The doctrine of instant sanctification at death has certain values. One sees that it is important to live for Christ in this life and it becomes a serious matter to postpone this decision. It is in harmony with the Protestant doctrine of justification by faith—the belief that a person's salvation depends on faith in God and cannot be earned by anything he does. But this doctrine too has been made subject to certain abuses. Since it makes no difference when the person accepts Christ, Public Enemy Number One who accepts Christ in the death house a few hours before electrocution can sweep into the Pearly Gates alongside a saintly philanthropist who gave his whole life to the service of Christ. It doesn't seem just for a sinner who repents during a lingering illness to be saved while no worse a sinner is lost because he dies suddenly. Also the view of instant sanctification condemns the heathen to everlasting punishment because they did not accept Christ. It would seem just to all that they have an opportunity to accept him, if not in this life then in the next. Some modern Christians think there is a place of probation for those who have no proper probation on the earth.

WHAT SHALL WE BELIEVE?—What, then, shall we believe in regard to eternal rewards and punishments?[17] The Bible, especially the teachings of Jesus, is very clear on one point: God will render to every man according to his works.

---

[17] Perhaps rewards and punishments are the wrong words to use. One does not want to be accused of doing a good deed in order to get a reward. However, one is happy when he does something which turns out all right. We can think of reward in that sense.

The law of the harvest is operative in the spiritual and moral realm.[18] Beyond that the Bible is not very definite. It does not tell us how God will reward or punish. Perhaps it is best that we do not know definitely. The terrors one knows not of are more terrifying than those that are known. But that lack of information does not keep us from thinking.

Let us consider the three views we find in the New Testament concerning the fate of the wicked. The first is that of eternal punishment.[19] The doctrine of eternal punishment was once useful in scaring people into a confession of Christ and in holding them to a straight and narrow way. Today it has largely lost its force. Perhaps it is just as well. It is not in harmony with the idea of the goodness of God. If punishment is not remedial it has no value. How can it be remedial if it is eternal? —if a person could never get out of torment to try to live aright? The Christian belief in a good God seems to forbid us to believe in any form of punishment that does not give us another chance. Whatever we may think, people today are not very much disturbed by the preaching of eternal punishment.

Other Christians believe that eventually everyone will be saved.[20] There is a great deal to be said for this idea that Christ will draw men unto Himself.[21] According to this view God loves everyone and is able to save all. Some people feel that God is not just unless He punishes people for their sins. They suggest that the righteous will serve God because they want to. The wicked will serve God against their will. This view, however, seems to leave man no opportunity to make a choice for himself. There is no real freedom if at last it is decreed that we shall do God's will whether willingly or unwillingly.

[18] Galatians 6:7.
[19] Matthew 25:41, 46.
[20] I Corinthians 15:22. See also John 12:32 and Romans 5:18.
[21] John 12:32.

The third view which we discover in the New Testament is that of destruction. Those who are wicked will be as though they had never been.[22] This is held by some Christians, but others object to it on the ground that a loving God could not destroy those whom He had made.

Thus it can be seen that not all Christians agree. One might suggest a combination of these three views. Those who are woefully wicked may be destroyed, while those who are perfectly good (how small a company!) will live in eternal bliss. Then the question arises as to what should be done with the rest of humanity. I have a friend who likes to quote, "We are punished not for our sins, but by our sins." It is the law of the harvest again, "Whatsoever a man soweth that shall he also reap." Shall one ever cease to regret the consequences of the lie that was told? Shall one ever forget the tear-stained face of a dear one after he has spoken angry words? It is possible, of course, that in the next world we shall not remember what happened in this world. But would it be heaven if we did not retain the values which are achieved on earth in terms of friendship and love, in terms of the creation of beauty, in terms of the accumulation of knowledge? And if a person remembers the values shall he not also remember his misdeeds?

More terrifying than a hell of fire and brimstone would be the prospect of remorse through eternity that one had caused the destruction of a human soul because one had not guided its infant feet where it should go, or that one had crushed some life by despair because one's greed had robbed him of an opportunity to earn his daily bread. One may ask what hope of happiness may be left under such a view. There is the hope that the evil and greedy and selfish part of his life recedes into the past and has less and less effect upon his

[22] II Thessalonians 1:9; Matthew 7:13; Hebrews 10:26-27.

happiness. The words of Jesus are vibrant with the hope that the right shall eventually triumph.

WHAT IS THE NEXT WORLD LIKE?—Most people are curious about the nature of the life beyond the grave. Some are likely to think of the next world as a material world like this. A farmer asked his pastor what kind of a place heaven was, saying that he had heard that heaven was a city—that if that were true he didn't want to go there, because he liked the country. But the teachings of Jesus and Paul give no evidence that it is a physical existence. In the resurrection, people do not marry.[23] Flesh and blood have no part in the kingdom of God.[24] The invalid who rejoiced that she was nothing but skin and bones missed the point. If the life beyond the grave is a spiritual existence how do we live without bodies? The Greeks at Corinth, who believed that the body was the enemy of the soul, said that they did not believe in the resurrection of the body. Paul at once defended the doctrine of the resurrection of the body, but he spoke of a spiritual body which should be as different from the physical body as the new stalk of wheat is different from the grain which is placed in the ground. However, he did not give a very clear idea of what he meant by the spiritual body. Perhaps we can infer that he thought of it as being free from certain limitations which the physical body puts upon men.

With what will a person occupy himself in the life that is to be? Perhaps there is reason to believe that there will be an opportunity for achievement. Jesus indicated that the kingdom of heaven would grow.[25] If that is true, then there will be a chance for service on the other side. There is an ancient tradition that when God made the first paradise he put man in it to tend it.[26] Maybe it is characteristic of paradises that

[23] Matthew 22:30.
[24] I Corinthians 15:50.
[25] Mark 4:28.
[26] Genesis 2:15.

they need caretaking. Maybe work is essential to happiness. Whatever the life beyond is like, Christians look for it to climax a life of faith and hope and love.

FOR DISCUSSION

1. What forces caused modern man to transfer his interest from the life to come to this life? In what ways has this change of emphasis benefited man? Harmed him?
2. How many persons that you know would be willing to die for a good cause, if they believed death were the end of all? Does a belief in immortality actually inspire one to nobler living?
3. Is it necessary to give up this world to win the next? Give reasons for your answer.
4. Must the man or woman of scientific pursuit or interest give up his belief in personal immortality? Explain.
5. Select the reasons for believing in immortality which appeal most to you and attempt to explain them to someone else in your own words.
6. What belief about the place of the wicked and of the righteous in the next life would lead to the most ethical lives?
7. What belief about the fate of the bad and of the good would be most consistent with the Christian idea of God?

CHAPTER 9

What Is the Place of the Church?

A. What Is the Church?

Most likely you belong to a church, because about half the American people do. You are acquainted with the building, the Bible School Hall or Parish Hall, the social parlors, and the parsonage or rectory or manse. No doubt you have heard members refer to your church in a very kindly way. Many who belong to the church love it very much. For that reason they sometimes criticize it, but more often they speak well of it and want to see it grow. They take pride in its appearance. They want it to be beautiful, comfortable, and adequate to the needs of the congregation.

It is rather easy to get the idea that a church is a building made of wood, stone, brick, and mortar. But, if that is the case, then what is the difference between a church and lodge hall or a mercantile building? So now we must consider what makes a church: How is it different from other institutions? What is Jesus' conception of the church?

THE CHURCH AS AN INSTITUTION.—The New Testament does not give any specific direction for the organization of the church. Jesus referred to the church [1] as something that will inevitably result from His teaching and spirit. The beginning of Christianity was a fellowship and the church as an institution grew naturally out of this fellowship.

The Roman Catholic conception of the church today is the institutional conception. It believes that man must be taught what to believe, how to live, and what he must do to be saved. According to it, Jesus gave his disciples the authority to guide men in these three phases of religion, an authority passed on through the ages until the present day. Thus God's will for man is expressed by the church and the church's voice is the final authority in all such matters. In this concept the church is of divine origin and it does not err. Its authority is final in all spiritual matters. It also reserves for itself the right to interpret the Word of God. This is the institutional conception of the Church that is believed and taught by the Roman Catholic Church.

These Roman Catholic beliefs concerning the church extend further. As an institution, it has the right to determine what a man should believe in order to be saved. [2] Just as Peter and the other Apostles had the authority to determine what was necessary for salvation, so the church has that authority yet today. [3] Jesus gave the authority of the keys of the Kingdom to Peter and that authority has been passed on from

[1] Matthew 16:18; 18:17. [3] Matthew 16:19.
[2] Acts 16:30, 31.

generation to generation until the present time. Only the church has the right to interpret the Word of God so that errors cannot creep in. The church is divinely appointed to do this work and its mission is to guide men on the way of salvation. In this it cannot err. Individuals may interpret the Word of God in many ways, but their interpretation is fallible. For that reason the Roman Church holds that any interpretation that is authoritative must come from the church. Of course, we understand that the institutional conception of the church is that it is composed of the Hierarchy. The Hierarchy is composed of the Pope, the cardinals, the bishops, the monsignori, and the priests. They, through official meetings, declare what the will of God is for man. These declarations are in various forms: encyclicals, edicts, bulls, and other official declarations to which the members of the church must conform if they would be saved.

This pertains also to life. The church as an institution has the right to declare how Christian people must live. All acts of life with a moral implication must be prescribed by the church. Such matters as marriage, divorce, attendance at mass and the sacraments, days of fasting, holy days, private devotions, forms of prayer, and other matters pertaining to the personal religious life are definitely stated by the church. These requirements help to achieve conformity and make it much easier for the member to know just what he must do in order to live a Christian life.

We mentioned before that the institutional conception of the church is a profession that Christ met man's religious needs by teaching what he must believe, how he must live, and how he can be saved. Jesus exercised three offices in showing this way: those of the prophet, the priest, and the Saviour. As the prophet, He spoke the will of God and preached it; as a priest, He was the intermediary between sinful man and God; as the Saviour, He was the all-sufficient sacrifice for man's sins. The church must exercise these three offices in His name. As the prophet, the church may tell men what to believe; as the priest, it is the intermediary between man and God; and as the Saviour, it presents the all-sufficient sacrifice that is reenacted daily in the Mass.

THE CHURCH AS A FELLOWSHIP.—Over against this view of the church as an institution stands the spiritual theory of the church. This conception of the church does not hold that it is a man-made institution, but that it is a divine expression of the spirit of Christ. Since Jesus himself did not set up a physical organization, the organization grew naturally out of the fellowship of the believers with one another and with God. The church, then, is a divine life that came into the world with Christ. The Spirit that He promised [4] is the guiding power of the church. This conception of the church places the final authority of the religious life upon the fellowship as it is guided by the spirit of Christ. It is not individualistic as some contend and does not give every individual the right to interpret the will of God as he sees fit. This misconception has caused many unfortunate divisions of the Protestant Church. We will consider these divisions in more detail a little later. But for the present let us say that the final authority in the Protestant Church is the Spirit of Christ as it is expressed in the fellowship of believers and as it lives in the Bible. Each fellowship is guided by its group or through its appointed representatives. These interpret the will of God for the individuals who are members of the fellowship. It is true that this spiritual fellowship expresses itself institutionally also. There are rituals, rules, and creeds but these are not handed down to individuals by higher authorities; rather they are formulated by the individuals through their representatives. These are not permanent nor are they considered

[4] John 14:18-31.

infallible; if the spiritual needs of the fellowship change, then these rituals, sermons, rules, and creeds can also be changed to meet these needs.

The spirit of Jesus in the lives of His followers is the guiding principle and final authority in the Protestant Church. The Bible is a source of authority and brings truth to the believer. The church must be considered then as something more than buildings, equipment, clergy, and officers. These are the visible expressions of the vital spirit of Christ. They are the means to an end and not an end in themselves. They are creations of the spirit to serve the needs of the fellowship. We notice in the New Testament that the first election of deacons [5] was the result of a necessity. The physical expression of the spirit of Christ grew beyond the ability of the Apostles to manage. The fellowship sensed the situation and chose deacons as assistants to the Apostles. These assistants were given the task of supervising the temporal affairs of the congregation so the Apostles could give themselves more fully to the spiritual ministry. In this we see that organization, or institution, grew out of the needs of the fellowship. In this manner various phases of the institutional life of the church had their origin.

The same can be said concerning the creeds and expressions of faith. They were formulated because there was a need for the Christians to express just what they believed. This need arose out of the desire to evangelize and to set minimum standards of faith for all who wanted to have a share in the fellowship. The Protestant Church holds that these creeds, since they are an expression of faith, can be changed or amended by the fellowship whenever it feels that they are not meeting the needs. The Protestant Church allows freedom of conscience in matters that are considered nonessential to salvation. For that reason there is a divergence of opinion in

[5] Acts 6:1–6.

the Protestant Church concerning certain types of amusement and entertainment. We also find various types of polity in the Protestant Church because polity is the expression of a need of the fellowship, and that which meets the need of a certain group does not necessarily meet the need of another. This again is nonessential to salvation, and is therefore the prerogative of any group of the fellowship. It may seem that the Protestant Church is greatly divided but upon closer examination we find that it is essentially united except on matters such as polity and custom. It is unfortunate that these nonessentials are all too often emphasized at the cost of unity of the spirit. Those who deal with members of every religious denomination soon find that the essentials of the faith are believed by all of them.

These then are the two conceptions of the church, the Institutional Idea as exemplified in the Roman Catholic Church, and the Fellowship Idea held by Protestants.

THE FUNCTION OF THE CHURCH.—Perhaps we can best understand what the church is if we study what it does. Anything should justify its existence by meeting needs, and the same may be said of the church. Jesus certainly did not come into the world merely to establish an organization. God's will is good and purposive and we see the expression of it in the life of Jesus. The church, which is the expression of Jesus' spirit, must be likewise good and purposive.

THE CHURCH SPEAKS FOR CHRIST.—When the Apostles received the divine commission [6] they were not equipped with any organization to promote their cause or give them financial aid. Ten days later [7] a realization came over them that they had a profound message and the Holy Spirit moved them to proclaim it. The important thing was that they had something to say that profoundly changed the lives of the people who

[6] Matthew 28:19-20.   [7] Acts 2:1-21.

heard it, and on the first Pentecost [8] three thousand were so deeply impressed by this message that they professed faith in Christ and asked for baptism. That message was so vital that in one generation it spread into every large city of the entire Roman Empire.

The message of the church is one that profoundly affects life. It meets the needs of the total personality of man. The materialistic emphasis of the first century left the impression that man lives by bread alone and that might is right. But in such a culture people could not find peace; the hunger of the soul was left unsatisfied. The Apostles came with the message that man is not a mere pawn in the hands of blind passion but a potential child of God and his life may be good and purposive. To proclaim this message is the first and probably the greatest function of the church.

The message of the church was revolutionary. It placed emphasis upon the divine right of the individual in a culture that claimed prerogatives for only a few. It is easily understood why political and religious authorities opposed a message as revolutionary as that. It knocked them out of their complacency. It developed conscience in the lives of those who identified themselves with the fellowship. It brought hope for the masses who had become bewildered and disillusioned.

The church came with this message of hope at a time when old foundations were crumbling. Belief in the ancient Roman and Greek gods had served its day and there were few intelligent people who still adhered to those faiths. Emperor worship was instituted in a vain attempt to unite the empire through a common religion. This resulted at most in a half-hearted formal observance, and since these faiths had resulted in nothing better than untold poverty for the great masses of people they never became vital forces of life. Morality

[8] Acts 2:41.

had reached an all-time low and the dignity of man was lost. It is true that pagan philosophers raised their voices in protest, but they had nothing vital to substitute. Then the church came with its message and men looked up again. The message filled the void in life and gave them ideals once more.

The message of the church is vital and of similar necessity today. We also live in a culture that is materialistic. It may be said that standards of living are important and that there should be no excuse for poverty and starvation in a world of plenty. The fact still holds, however, that man does not live by bread alone. Certainly we want to see economic conditions bettered, human suffering alleviated, just and equitable conditions existing in human relationships; but even though these ideals may be achieved, they will not satisfy all the needs of man because man is more than a physical body. There is plenty of room for improvement in these conditions in the world today and many persons are horrified by the selfishness and greed that still motivate men in their relationships with one another. But even though these conditions be remedied, the needs of the soul must still be met.

Christ speaks to man through the message of His church. Through the ages the church has preserved that message and offers it to humanity now. The voice of Jesus gives us hope, even in a day when the world is torn by prejudice and hatred. Its message says that in spite of the hatred instilled in men's hearts by war and selfishness we still have the right to say "Our Father." This message teaches us that the world is not unfriendly to human life. We have made it that way against the will of God, but it need not necessarily be so. When the spirit of Christ is permitted to have its way the dignity of man is restored. Life can be good and it can be purposive; it can have meaning and hope.

The message of the church lifts man out of selfishness. It causes him to see the common good. The great masses of people are still motivated by selfishness and for that reason we have much unhappiness. But the spirit of Christ is like the leavening of the loaf.[9] Here and there we see evidences of its power, but certainly not to the extent that we will some day. Its message is one of justice, faith, love, and hope. This is what men need today more than any other thing.

THE RITES AND RITUALS OF THE CHURCH.—The church also meets man's spiritual needs through rites, rituals, and forms of worship. It is the function of the church to aid man in his approach to God. The sacraments were instituted by Christ himself for this purpose. But as the church grew in organization and as men of all races, nationalities, and temperaments came within its portals, it became the purpose of the church to meet the varied spiritual needs. That is why the church is "catholic"; it can meet the spiritual needs of all people. The sacraments were supplemented by rites and rituals and forms of worship to meet these needs. The sacraments, as we said, were instituted by Christ. In the Protestant Church there are two of these, Baptism and Holy Communion. The Roman Catholic Church observes seven: Baptism, Communion, Confirmation, Confession and Penance, Marriage, Extreme Unction, and Holy Orders. The Protestant Church aids man in worship by providing consecration services, inspirational services, the use of hymns, rituals, musical instruments, church architecture, and other things. At the present time there is a trend toward beauty in the Protestant Church. Immediately following the Reformation, Protestantism swung to an extreme asceticism in protest against the use of images, and churches became bare and ugly. In a similar protest against the mass, many denominations shunned all ritual and the church worship became opening exercises. The entire emphasis was laid upon preaching and fellowship.

[9] Luke 13:20–21.

Today we see a trend in the direction of aiding man in worship through the restoration of beauty in the church. Where the pulpit formerly was the center of attraction, in our later Protestant churches the altar has assumed that place. Symbolic stained glass windows, candelabra, crosses, and beautiful paintings, as well as other symbolic art, are appearing more generally in the Protestant church. Accompanying this trend toward beauty is a tendency toward increased dignity in the order of worship. In the rituals, the classic prayers and invocations are being used. And by this means the worshiper feels a fellowship with the saints of the past as well as the present. The beauty of the house of God serves the purpose of lifting man out of the ugliness of everyday life. As a matter of fact, the beauty of the church is sometimes just about the only beauty in the lives of some of the people who worship there.

The use of classic hymns is also an aid to worship. Preserved for us by the church, they are things of lasting beauty. There are some Protestant denominations in which the classic hymns are quite unknown and more modern songs are used. Some of these have very catchy melodies and are easy to sing and sometimes even tickle the toes. There is a question whether it is advisable for Christians to use these songs in worship services, but because they are easy to sing many people like them. Conservatively speaking, we can say that these songs should not be used because their messages and melodies suggest the sensuous rather than the spiritual. When dying is compared to a train pulling into a railroad station and heaven is to be desired because there are no taxes there, we are putting our spiritual life on a pretty low level. The hymn books of the more conservative denominations in most instances omit these songs. It is the business of the church to lift men higher, not to cater to the desires of the body.

Our daily life is quite a harried affair. Our economic system makes it very hard to earn a living, and in order to exist in this world with a decent standard of living adult members of the family quite generally have to keep their noses to the grindstone. Our scramble for existence is a challenge, and we all need help in bringing God into daily living. That is what the church is here to do. It must make God real and available. If it fails in this, it is not functioning as it should. The order of worship in the church is designed with this purpose in view. There, in the fellowship with believers, the worshiper is also brought into a fellowship with God. Some phases of the order of worship, such as the confession of faith, the hymns, and the prayers, bring us into fellowship with one another as the children of a common Father. In the educational program of the church the Word of God is taught and the traditions, customs, and beliefs of the church are transmitted from one generation to another. In this manner the individual is prepared to participate intelligently and spiritually in the more formal worship services of the church. The curricula of these teaching institutions of the church are designed to lead the individual into active church membership and provide him with the spiritual and cultural background that he needs in order to join the fellowship as it worships.

Another function of the church is to direct man to useful service. There is no special merit in just being good; the person must be good for something. The church directs the energies of man into useful pursuits. God gives us talents to use, and if they are not used they are lost just as an arm grows weak when it is not exercised.

Since religion deals with all phases of life, so the church is concerned about all man's interests. Somehow the mistaken impression has developed that the church is interested only in the soul of man. Man's spiritual welfare is the major concern of the church. But the spiritual involves his temporal welfare also. So the church, through its organizations, engages in all kinds of social service. In this it practices historical Christianity. Jesus frequently pointed out the difficulties of the poor, the unfortunate, and the sick, and did something for them. The early disciples followed Jesus' example.[10] They established institutions called xenodochia for the care of the sick, the stranger, the insane, and the poor. The church still engages in such philanthropy; it maintains homes for the orphans, the aged, the feeble-minded, and the epileptics, and builds hospitals for the care of the sick. Every recognized denomination has a commission on benevolent institutions through which the individual members engage in social service.

Through its organizations or committees, the church promotes Christian citizenship.[11] The church member is taught how to be a good citizen of his community, his nation, and the world. Sometimes there is a conflict of ideals, and in such instances the Christian will love his nation and do all that he can to make the ideals of his nation such that he can live there with a clear conscience. In this he will not sacrifice his Christian principles.

The church is mission-minded. Through its national missions program it reaches into the densely populated sections and rapidly growing new sections of great cities and the sparsely populated areas of rural districts where it attempts to meet the spirituals needs of the people. This work is supported by direct giving or by the activities of various organizations within the church. Through international missions the church reaches out into foreign countries. Missionary societies and direct giving support this work. Because the church carries on a widespread program of evangelization, there is scarcely a country on earth today where the name of

[10] James 1:27.   [11] Hebrews 13:17; I Peter 2:13, 14.

Jesus is not known. There are also such church-related missionary movements as the American Bible Society that are interdenominational. These supplement the program of the churches and are supported financially by a number of churches.

The church is an ambassador of good will. In a world that is divided by racial, national, and social antagonisms, the church comes with a message of love and reconciliation. Jesus emphasized the importance of love in human relations. As a matter of fact, he made it the sign and badge of Christianity.[12]

Hatred brings death. Nation pitted against nation, race against race, and class against class cause conflict, and the ensuing results are disastrous. Governments are established to assure the safety of life and property, but as long as hatred is in men's hearts governments will be ineffective in achieving this objective. For this reason, even though people pay a tremendous price for government, thus far they have not been getting their money's worth. That the history of man is the story of one war after another demonstrates that government has not met the need, neither is it capable by itself of meeting the need. There are many who have come to the conclusion that, as far as man's safety is concerned, human government has literally failed. The reason for the failure lies not so much in organization or politics as in the motives that prompt men. The church, if it is loyal to the spirit of Jesus, will rise above the hatreds and prejudices that divide the human family and attempt to unite mankind in a common brotherhood. It is the function of the church to promote good will among men and thus aid government to preserve peace and protect life and property.

God does not favor one race or nationality over another, and in Jesus Christ we can break down the barriers that divide men. The early disciples recognized this fundamental

[12] John 13:35.

message of Christianity.[13] As this spirit of Jesus motivates ever more men, it will become possible for people to live together in peace and good will.

To love a friend and to hate an enemy have no special merit. Anyone is capable of these; such ethics are on the pagan level. Christianity presents ideals that are worthy of effort to attain.[14] To love your enemies is not easy, but it is worth trying because it brings results that can be attained in no other way. It also brings social and economic benefits as rewards for such effort.

The least that can be expected of Christians is that they live together harmoniously. While it is true that Christians are human, it is also true that there is no excuse for the pettiness that sometimes characterizes their actions. This is a denial of the spirit of Jesus, and the true Christian recognizes his weakness and strives ever to attain higher goals of achievement in Christian relations. The spirit of Jesus is something very exacting, but it is worth the effort. The church must proclaim and live Jesus' message of love.

It is the function of the church to proclaim Jesus.[15] This statement is rather general and implies very much. To proclaim Jesus means more than to preach about Him, although that is essential. The church must teach what Jesus taught, but more than that it must emphasize Christian living. Teaching what Jesus taught implies the use of various methods, of which the preaching is the most important. Other methods of teaching are followed in the programs of the various societies, organizations, and educational institutions of the church. The content of Jesus' message and the meaning of His life must be a focal point of all this activity. He must be the Foundation, the Head, and the Cornerstone of the spiritual structure of the church.[16]

---

[13] Galatians 3:28.
[14] Matthew 5:44.

[15] I Corinthians 1:23; 2:2.
[16] Ephesians 2:20.

The import of the message of Jesus for the individual and for society is the program of the church. All its activity and all its agencies receive their inspiration from Him.

B. The Church and the Churches

We have spoken of the church as a vital fellowship. It seems paradoxical that this fellowship should be so divided. The two major groups in Christianity are the Catholic and the Protestant groups. The Catholic group is divided into Eastern (orthodox) and Western (Roman) and Coptic. The Protestants are divided into many groups. *The Year Book of American Churches* [17] lists 256 religious bodies with 253,762 churches and 72,492,669 members. This includes the Roman Catholic Church which has 14,791 churches and 23,419,701 members. That leaves 49,072,968 members of the Protestant churches. We must bear in mind, however, that this figure does not include a large number of Protestant bodies of which no statistics are available. The 256 religious bodies do include a large number of very small denominations. Seventy million Christians belong to fifty-five of the larger religious bodies that have over fifty thousand members each. In other words 97.4 per cent of the church membership in the United States belongs to the larger church bodies and 2.6 per cent of the membership is found in 201 small denominations.

An analysis of the situation leads to the conclusion that the church has a tremendous task confronting it: a task of uniting its own forces. Because it is divided, the church cannot speak as a common witness to Christ. This is borne out in almost any community that is overchurched, with little groups struggling to maintain themselves and often engaging in competitive activities. Such action weakens the voice of the

[17] *Year Book of American Churches,* Sowers Ptg. Co., Lebanon, Pa., 1945.

church, even in regard to its own members. For instance, when an individual needs the discipline of the church, there is a tendency for him to leave it and to be accepted with open arms in another competitive body. Instead of unity in facing man's common foe, sin, the church thus stands relatively impotent.

Many divisions have arisen through varied interpretations of the Scripture, or through an emphasis upon nonessentials. As far as such occurrences within individual churches are concerned, there are many examples that could be cited. When the individual communion glasses were first being widely used, a congregation considered purchasing such a communion set. The decision was made by a majority vote. The minority group withdrew and started another church because they did not want individual communion glasses. Today both churches are using individual communion cups but both small congregations, though struggling for existence, still refuse to unite.

The things that disrupt the fellowship of Christians are usually nonessential to Salvation. It is true that many of us are very unkind to God, and instead of fashioning ourselves after God's image we try to narrow God to our own pettiness. One of the great tasks of this day is to work for greater unity in the church, but this cannot be achieved so long as influential leaders in the denominations assume that their way is the only way to Salvation.

In the last twenty-five years we have seen a very promising growth toward Christian fellowship. We are beginning to realize that loyalty to one denomination does not necessarily imply that the others are wrong. Many older people were raised in such strict denominationalism that in their childhood they were actually taught that members of other churches were doomed. How could they get a different impression when they heard the minister pray that the people of the

United Brethren, or the Baptist, or the Methodist, or what-have-you church "be converted from their evil ways and live?"

There is no need to gloss over the divisions in the church. While there are many who are devoting their lives to the establishment of a better understanding, there are still many who refuse to be moved. The division between the Roman Catholic and the Protestant churches is still very great. The clergymen refuse to unite their forces for a common good. In most cities there is a ministerial alliance of the Protestant ministers. They meet periodically and discuss programs of mutual interest, but it is hard to get any kind of a united statement even from this group. Even such a matter as a public gathering of paper for the war effort on Sunday could not draw forth a common statement. When the Women's Federation of the various denominations wanted to hold a World Day of Prayer Service and close it with Holy Communion, the objections from certain pastors were so vehement that it could not be done. One minister said, and he represented a large denomination, that he would have to ask the members of his church not to participate because they could take Communion only in the church of their denomination. The Lord's Table is, for them, a "closed shop." In the midst of this disunion is there any hope that the fellowship will ever be united? [18] Let us see.

TRENDS TOWARD ORGANIC UNION.—There are two ways in which the fellowship may be strengthened. The one is by organic union, or merger, and the other is through strengthening the bonds of fellowship and understanding. As far as organic union (merger) is concerned, church bodies with a similar heritage have been tending toward organic union since the turn of the century. Some of these unions or mergers have been effected. The Presbyterian Church in the U.S.A. and the Cumberland Presbyterian Church united about 1908

[18] John 17:22.

to form the Presbyterian Church in the U.S.A. Although a number of the Cumberland Churches have not entered the merger, it has been largely effective. In Canada the Methodist, the Presbyterian, and the Congregational Churches united in 1935 to form the United Church of Canada. The Congregational and the Christian Churches in the United States united to form the Congregational Christian Church. The Evangelical Synod of North America and the Reformed Church in the United States united to form the Evangelical and Reformed Church. The Methodist Episcopal Church South, the Methodist Episcopal Church, and the Methodist Protestant Church merged into the Methodist Church. The Evangelical and the United Brethren denominations united to form the Evangelical United Brethren Church. There are other examples of such mergers and unions. Some Lutheran bodies have merged, and today there are other bodies aiming in that direction. The Congregational Christian Church and Evangelical and Reformed Church are talking of merger. The Presbyterian Church in the United States is having conversations with the Episcopal Church and the United Presbyterian Church of North America. So we see that denominations with similar heritages are tending toward union. This tendency seems to be confined more to the larger denominations. We believe the spirit may be caught by other groups of similar background and heritage and in the coming years more mergers and unions will be effected, which will lower the number of Protestant denominations and tend to give the Protestant Church the ability to speak with a more united voice.

TRENDS IN SPIRITUAL FELLOWSHIP.—Aside from the tendency toward actual union or merger, there is the tendency toward fellowship in the spirit between the various denominations of Protestantism. The Federal Council of the

Churches of Christ in America now has, according to the 1945 *Year Book,* twenty-five constituent bodies from the following groups: Brethren, Congregational, Disciples, Episcopal, Evangelical, Friends, Lutheran, Methodist, Moravian, Orthodox, Presbyterian, Reformed, and the United Church of Canada. These include a total of 27,749,967 members. The Federal Council of the Churches of Christ in America is a part of the World Council of Churches with headquarters in Geneva, Switzerland. It is interesting to note that at the inception of World War II the World Council of Churches was in the process of formation. Just when the political world was disintegrating the Christian Church was uniting. This world organization of the Church represents eighty-eight denominations in twenty-three different countries and is constantly growing. World conferences have been held: one at Stockholm in 1925, another at Lausanne, Switzerland, in 1927, one at Oxford in 1937, and another immediately following at Edinburgh in the same year. In these conferences steps were taken to organize and establish the World Council of Churches, which came officially into existence in the summer of 1939. It is very significant that this move was made in Christianity just before the outbreak of World War II. "Ecumenicity," a ponderous word, is becoming familiar; the term describes the Christian Church as a united world agency. A provisional committee with vice-chairmen in Paris, London, New York, and Geneva guided the destinies of the World Council during the war.

The last thirty years have seen a steady growth in spiritual fellowship. In nearly all cities, ecumenical services in which most of the Protestant denominations cooperate are held at least once a year. Union services on such great occasions as Thanksgiving, World Day of Prayer, and Reformation Sunday are held in which denominational emphases are not stressed but rather the spirit of unity is proclaimed.

Through the World Council of Churches the various denominations are uniting to meet the needs of a suffering world. Immediately following World War II, church leaders from various parts of the world assembled at Geneva, Switzerland, and formed an interdenominational staff to direct relief for the churches of Europe. Among those present were Stuart W. Hermann, Jr., formerly pastor of the American Church in Berlin, whose duty it was to direct the reconstruction of church life in Germany, Yugoslavia, Rumania, and Bulgaria. Dr. Benjamin J. Bush, former pastor of Westminster Church in Detroit, Michigan, was in charge of aid to theological education throughout Europe and worked among the churches of Belgium, Holland, Czechoslovakia, and Hungary. Dr. S. C. Michelfelder, pastor of the largest Church of the American Lutheran denomination at Toledo, Ohio, was the delegate from the American section of the Lutheran World Convention. He directed the cooperation between his communion and the World Council in relief work. Mr. Robert W. Root, reporter and editorial writer of Des Moines, Iowa, interpreted the needs of the European churches and the relief activities of the United States. In addition to these the Rev. Werner Wickstrom of the Methodist Church, the Rev. Ewart W. Turner of the Religious News Service, Dr. Robbins Barstow, and Dr. Samuel McCrea Cavert, secretary of the Federal Council in America, conferred with church leaders in Geneva, Paris, and London for the purpose of planning reconstruction. Dr. Carl E. Schneider was the representative of the Evangelical and Reformed Church on the staff of the Department of Reconstruction of the World Council in Geneva.

Even though the World Council was in the process of formation at the outbreak of World War II, it had progressed to such an extent that it could exist in the name of Protestantism and of the Eastern Orthodox Church during the years of the war. Services to prisoners of war, relief distribution to the destitute and to exiled pastors, and the exchange of evidences of unbroken fellowship across the lines of war were maintained. Even in the heat and hate of war the Church demonstrated its oneness in fellowship. And now that World War II is over the Christians in Europe and Asia are made to understand that the Christians the world over have not broken fellowship with them. Large sums of money are raised in America for rehabilitation work by all leading denominations. This great sum is administered wisely by the World Council. All of this points to a better appreciation of Christianity, not as an institution, but as a Christian fellowship.

Looking Ahead.—The glory of the church is not what it was, but rather what it is and what it can become. The Christian Church commands the respect of thinking people today more than at any other time. It has passed through the storm and stress of another World War and weathered the storm magnificently. In World War I the church became confused and lent itself to the influences of the day through patriotic pressure. Many sanctuaries were used as places of recruitment and for the sale of bonds, and were used generally to whoop up the war spirit. Many conscientious clergymen who refused to use the church for these purposes were ostracized and otherwise humiliated. There was no voice of the church strong enough to be heard in protest against such treatment.

Church leaders learned many lessons from this experience and were not so easily swept along by the war spirit in the more recent conflict. The years taught that wars do not bring Utopia upon the earth, but rather that they are a hellish business. Economic and political states are formulated by diplomats and politicians, not by the men who win victories on the field of battle, and the church learned from bitter experience that wars are rather futile. If the Kingdom of God is to come upon the earth it will not be brought by bloodshed, destruction, and obliteration of peoples. In these years we learned that the human race has not developed spiritually beyond the possibility of barbarism. The church had deluded itself into thinking that man could not debase himself beneath the status of a jungle beast. It was rudely shocked to a realization that political authorities can lead large sections of people to a psychological condition where they are capable of ruthlessly exterminating thousands of innocent people. Ghettos and concentration camps, prisons and other horrible means were used to exterminate people who exercised their privilege to think or in whose veins certain racial bloods flowed. The church was rudely awakened to the fact that its work on earth is not by any means finished and that the greatest possibilities of achievement are yet to be realized.

The church in Britain and America did not let pressure cause it to praise war this time. The church proclaimed war to be the arch-enemy of mankind. The church prayed the blessing of God upon the young men and young women who, through no fault of their own, had to engage in the hellish business, sacrifice their young lives, disrupt their normal ways of living and, in millions of instances, become cripples for life. The church prayed for the mothers and fathers, the wives and the sweethearts of those upon whom their civilization brought this visitation. It declared in all humility that we are a sinful people and that its mission is not yet accomplished or this would never have been brought upon the earth.

Thousands of ministers volunteered for service as chaplains in the armed forces and this time refused to act as mail boys and lackies, but rather became the spiritual advisors of those who needed their guidance and counsel. The church kept in touch with the men and women who were away from home and remained a powerhouse of strength and inspiration for those who came to worship; the results were seen in the attendance. There was a marked increase in attendance in nearly all churches simply because they were meeting the primary spiritual needs of the people.

Through all the stress of the conflict the church continued to preach the message of the Saviour and the inherent brotherhood of man. It tried to keep faith with Christian people the world over, even those in Germany, Japan, and other countries with which we were at war. This is because the bond of fellowship knows no limitations of race or nationality. It is a bond that is universal.

Now that World War II is over and it is again possible for the church to function internationally, it is hastening to its task with a speed unprecedented in history. Through its world organizations it was functioning in far places a few months after the war, aiding in reconstruction, feeding the hungry—in short, like the Good Samaritan, pouring oil and wine into the wounds of a bleeding world. In 1948 a world conference of the Protestant and Eastern Orthodox Churches was held in Amsterdam, Holland, where leading churchmen of the world gathered to guide the thinking and planning of the church for the future. The church that is so old is revitalized by the spirit of Jesus and no one can say what is yet to be or just what important part the church will play in the future destinies of mankind.

Today the church is alive to its task, more so than it has ever been before. Crusades for Christ are being conducted in the major communions. There is a renewed interest in personal evangelism, in Christian stewardship, and Christian education. More and more laymen are being enlisted in the program of evangelism, and it appears that the church will grow in members and spiritual power in the years ahead.

The church is the conscience of society and will be increasingly recognized as such as time goes on. As a conscience it awakens us to an awareness of the conditions and customs that trouble society. It is a means of raising the aspirations of the community and cannot be placated by any bribery. It promotes ideals by which man can live and enjoy the destiny that God intends for him in this world and the next.

Someone has said that the church is an anvil that has worn out many hammers. The ages verify that statement. Today after almost two thousand years it is more vital than ever before and stands in a position to play a great role in guiding the destiny of man in future generations. One thing is certain, it will always protect the rights of God's children and oppose anything that would rob mankind of its birthright.

FOR DISCUSSION

1. Do you think the Church should be concerned with economics and politics?
2. Do you think that some of the criticisms of the Church have bases in facts: for instance, that its ideas and practices are outmoded?
3. What is the Roman Catholic conception of the Church as an institution?
4. Discuss the Protestant conception of the Church as a fellowship.
5. Does the Protestant Church suffer because it lacks authority? What is its authority? What is the authority in the Roman Catholic Church?
6. Are creeds expressions of what Christians believe or are they statements that Christians must believe?
7. What is the function of the Church?
8. How do rites, rituals, and forms of worship help man in his approach to God?
9. What is the Federal Council of Churches of Christ in America? Does it function in your city?

10. What is the World Council of Churches? What is it doing now?
11. Discuss some mergers or unions of denominations. Do you know any other trends toward organic union?
12. What is the difference between spiritual fellowship and organic union?
13. Do you think the Protestant Church is progressing in the direction of spiritual fellowship? Is that tendency commendable?

BIBLIOGRAPHY

Andrews, M. E. "God's Continuing Revelation." *Journal of Bible and Religion,* February, 1939.

Barry, F. R. *What Has Christianity to Say?* New York, Harper & Bros., 1937.

Bennett, J. C. *Christian Realism.* New York, Chas. Scribner's Sons, 1941.

Bennett, J. C. "The Christian Conception of Man." *Liberal Theology.* Edited by B. E. Roberts and H. P. Van Dusen. New York, Chas. Scribner's Sons, 1942.

Bevan, Edwyn. *Christianity.* New York, Henry Holt & Co., Inc., 1932.

Bowie, W. R. *The Bible.* New York, Association Press, 1940.

Bratton, F. D. "Origin, the First Christian Liberal." *Journal of Bible and Religion,* August, 1940.

Brightman, E. S. *The Finding of God.* New York, Abingdon-Cokesbury Press, 1931.

Brightman, E. S. *The Problem of God.* New York, Abingdon-Cokesbury Press, 1930.

Brightman, E. S. *Religious Values.* New York, Abingdon-Cokesbury Press, 1925.

Brown, William A. *How to Think of Christ.* New York, Chas. Scribner's Sons, 1945.

Buttrick, G. A. *Prayer.* New York, Abingdon-Cokesbury Press, 1942.

Cavert, S. M. "The New Place of the Church in Protestant Thinking." *Religion in Life,* Winter, 1939, New York, Abingdon-Cokesbury Press.

Coffin, H. S. "The Scriptures." *Liberal Theology.* Edited by D. E. Roberts and H. P. Van Dusen. New York, Chas. Scribner's Sons, 1942.

Colwell, Ernest Cadman. *An Approach to the Teaching of Jesus.* New York, Abingdon-Cokesbury Press, 1947.

Craig, Clarence T. *The Beginning of Christianity.* New York, Abingdon-Cokesbury Press, 1942.

Craig, Clarence T., ed. "The Challenge of Our Culture." *Interseminary Series,* Vol. I. New York, Harper & Bros., 1946–47.

Day, A. E. *Jesus and Human Personality.* New York, Abingdon-Cokesbury Press, 1934.

Denny, W. B. *The Career and Significance of Jesus Christ.* New York, Thomas Nelson & Sons, 1933.

Drake, D. *The Problems of Religion.* Boston, Houghton Mifflin Co., 1916.

Ferre, Nels F. S. "A Theological Doctrine of Man." *Religion in Life,* Autumn, 1942, New York, Abingdon-Cokesbury Press.

Ferre, Nels F. S. "The Meaning of Jesus for Modern Theology." *Christendom,* Winter, 1939.

Fosdick, H. E. *A Guide to Understanding the Bible.* New York, Harper & Bros., 1938.

Fosdick, H. E. *As I See Religion.* New York, Harper & Bros., 1932.

Gilkey, James G. *God Will Help You.* New York, The Macmillan Co., 1943.

Johnson, Paul E. *Psychology of Religion.* New York, Abingdon-Cokesbury Press, 1945.

Jones, E. S. *Christ and Human Suffering.* New York, Abingdon-Cokesbury Press, 1940.

Kepler, Thomas A. *Contemporary Religious Thought.* New York, Abingdon-Cokesbury Press, 1941.

Knudson, A. C. *The Doctrine of God.* New York, Abingdon-Cokesbury Press, 1930.

Latourette, Kenneth S., ed. "The Gospel, The Church and the World." *Interseminary Series,* Vol. III, New York, Harper & Bros., 1946-47.

Leiper, Henry Smith. *Christianity Today.* New York, Morehouse-Gorham Co., Inc., 194;.

MacIntosh, Douglas C. "Eternal Life." *Liberal Theology.* Edited by D. E. Roberts and H. P. Van Dusen. New York, Chas. Scribner's Sons, 1942.

MacIntosh, Douglas C. *Personal Religion.* New York, Chas. Scribner's Sons, 1942.

Matthews, W. R. "The Influence of the Bible upon the English Nations." *Journal of Bible and Religion,* February, 1939, National Association of Bible Instructors.

Miller, Carl Wallace. *A Scientist's Approach to Religion.* New York, The Macmillan Co., 1947.

Miller, Randolph C., ed. "The Church and Organized Movements." *Interseminary Series,* Vol. II. New York, Harper & Bros., 1946-47.

Mould, E. W. K. *Essentials of Bible History.* New York, The Ronald Press Co., 1939.

Nagler, A. W. *The Church in History.* New York, Abingdon-Cokesbury Press, 1929.

Nichols, James Hastings. *Primer for Protestants.* New York, Association Press, 1947.

Nolde, O. Frederick, ed. "Toward World-Wide Christianity." *Interseminary Series,* Vol. IV, New York, Harper & Bros., 1946-47.

Rall, H. F. *Christianity.* New York, Chas. Scribner's Sons, 1940.

Robinson, H. W. *Suffering, Human and Divine.* New York, The Macmillan Co., 1939.

Scott, M. J. *Jesus as Men Saw Him.* New York, P. J. Kenedy & Sons, 1940.

Skinner, C. R. *Liberalism Faces the Future.* New York, The Macmillan Co., 1937.

Soares, T. G. *Three Typical Beliefs.* Chicago, University of Chicago Press, 1937.

Speers, W. C., et al. *Laymen Speaking.* (Prominent laymen speak their mind on church and faith.) New York, Association Press, 1947.

Stewart, George. *The Church.* New York, Association Press, 1938.

Streeter, B. H. *Reality.* New York, The Macmillan Co., 1926.

Studdert-Kennedy, G. A. *The Wicket Gate.* London, Hodder & Stoughton, Ltd., 1932.

Swift, A. L., Jr. "Psychic Phenomena and Immortality." *Religion in Life,* Autumn, 1942, New York, Abingdon-Cokesbury Press.

Tittle, E. F. "God in History." *Christendom,* Winter, 1939, World Conference on Faith and Order.

Walker, Williston. *History of the Christian Church.* New York, Chas. Scribner's Sons, 1918.

Weatherhead, L. *Why Do Men Suffer?* London, Student Christian Movement Press, Ltd., 1939.

Wicks, R. R. *The Reason for Living.* New York, Chas. Scribner's Sons, 1934.

Van Dusen, H. P. *Reality & Religion.* New York, Association Press, 1940.

Van Dusen, H. P. "The Significance of Jesus Christ," *Liberal Theology.* Edited by D. E. Roberts and H. P. Van Dusen. New York, Chas. Scribner's Sons, 1942.

INDEX OF BIBLICAL REFERENCES

GENERAL INDEX

Acts, The, 8
Adam, 57
American Standard Version (See "Bible")
Amos, 3, 6
Anger, 16, 97, 98
Animal, 34, 81
Archeology and the Bible (See "Bible")
Asceticism, 75, 76
Athanasius, 9
Atheism, 62
Atonement, 83
Attitudes, 23, 92, 93
Authority, 14, 124, 126, 127, 129
  of Bible (See "Bible")

Babylonian exile, 4, 6
Baptism, 129, 131
Bible, 33, 34 (See also "Old Testament," "New Testament," "Prophets," "Scriptures," and the various books of the Bible.)
  American Standard Version, 7, 15
  archaeology and, 12
  authority of, 10, 11, 14
  Book of Life, 3
  how to study, 15–16
  indifference to, 12
  interpretation, 10
  irrelevance for today, 12–13
  King James Version, 7, 11
  and life situations, 9, 13
  manuscripts, 12
  new approach to, 13
  original languages of, 11
  Protestant view of, 11
  reasons for writing, 4
  science and, 12, 13–14
  translations, 11
  use by early church, 10
  use by Jesus, 9
  use, selective, 14

Bible—*Continued*
  use today, 11, 15, 16
  written Word of God, 3, 4
Blessed life, 110
Brotherhood of Man (See "Man")

Canonization,
  of New Testament (see "New Testament")
  of Old Testament (See "Old Testament")
Christ, 57, 58, 70, 77, 80, 115, 118, 119, 125, 137 (See also "Jesus")
  Blood, 81
  Church body of (See "Church")
  denial of humanity of, 79
  Divinity of, 79, 86
  from above, 84
  the Head, 84
  Priesthood of, 102
  primacy of, 28, 84, 136
  Second Coming, 8, 116
  significance of, 83
  spirit of, 126, 127, 131
  the Word, 84
Christian example, 79
Christian life, 73
Christians, 28
Christmas, 81
Church, 52, 81, 116, 123–147
  Body of Christ, 31, 85
  divisions of, 137, 138
  fellowship, 126–128
  function of, 128
  institution, 124
  membership, 137
  merger of, 139, 140
  Orthodox, 141, 142
  symbols of, 132
  union, 138–143
Citizenship, 6, 64, 111, 134, 135, 143
Commandments, Ten, 55, 56
Commentary, use of, 15
Commission, Divine, 128

DATE DUE